DELIUS

THE MAIN STREET AT GREZ-SUR-LOING
Delius's house on the left

DELIUS

BY

ARTHUR HUTCHINGS

PROFESSOR OF MUSIC
IN THE UNIVERSITY OF DURHAM

GREENWOOD PRESS, PUBLISHERS
WESTPORT, CONNECTICUT

Originally published in 1949
by Macmillan & Co., Ltd., London

First Greenwood Reprinting 1970

Library of Congress Catalogue Card Number 74-104289

SBN 8371-3958-9

Printed in the United States of America

DEDICATED

TO

CHARLES KENNEDY SCOTT

IN RECOGNITION OF HIS SERVICES
TO DELIUS'S CHORAL MUSIC
WITH THE PHILHARMONIC
CHOIR

ACKNOWLEDGMENTS

I wish to thank Mrs. Clare Delius-Black, Mrs. Mary Rowley, and Mr. Gordon Bryan for information about Delius and for the use of their photographs, Mr. Eric Fenby for satisfying me on points which only Delius's amanuensis could have confirmed, the proprietors of *The Musical Times* for permission to reprint from articles I had contributed to that periodical, and to Mr. Winton Dean for showing me several infelicities of style in the first impression of this book.

CONTENTS

PART ONE

BIOGRAPHICAL

PART TWO

A CRITICAL APPRECIATION
OF DELIUS'S MUSIC

CONTENTS

APPENDICES

LIST OF ILLUSTRATIONS

PART ONE

BIOGRAPHICAL

CHAPTER ONE

THE ADVENTURER

No artist's stature is finally measured by critics or practitioners in the same art, but by the extent and depth with which he expresses our common humanity during a long testing period. Ideally, all races and generations should be his witnesses, but in fact only the musically sensitive can judge a composer; only those with his own cultural tradition can fully appreciate his utterance. If for several generations, however, the general musical public of his cultural inheritance think him to be a giant, the estimate is likely to be reliable even when his musically learned contemporaries thought him a dwarf.

Since their deaths between the two great wars of our time, two English composers have survived this test; both appeal chiefly to the English, and one of them, Elgar, did so deliberately. Despite glaring idiosyncrasies and occasional banalities not found in slicker musicians with smaller aim, Delius and Elgar continue to tower head and shoulders above their gifted English contemporaries. It is right that a critical biography of Delius should wait some time after his death before claiming its subject's place in the roll of giants, and right that Elgar's name should be inscribed first, not because he was the greater artist (the present writer is among those who think he was not) but because it is hard to recall a single composer of Delius's standing who is so much a law unto himself, even among our insular musicians.

3

In the opinion of one critic, " his mannerisms stand out a mile ". Having reached maturity of expression, his style underwent no change — the mannerisms remained. Like Hotspur, he " tied his ear to no tongue but his own "; his favourite gramophone records were those of his own works; as man and artist he was obstinate. Yet, as Johnson wrote of Shakespeare, he " may now begin to assume the dignity of an ancient, and to claim the privilege of established right and prescriptive veneration ". Johnson's magniloquence is also pertinent to our delay in recognising Delius as one of the supreme masters, for " the irregular combinations of fanciful invention may delight awhile by that novelty of which the common satiety of life sends us all in quest: but the pleasures of sudden wonders are soon exhausted, and the mind can only repose upon the stability of truth ". Was not Delius a sudden wonder ? Were we not once intoxicated by a romantic technique that has since become the stock in trade of ephemeral music ? We place him with the masters to-day because, quite aware of, and used to, the technical decadence of his art-phase, we are also aware of a personality so powerful that the method is transcended even in works containing long stretches of drugged somnolence.

There are other proofs of Delius's stature. One is the fact that he found a uniquely individual musical language from influences which must have made a deep impression upon his early musical vocabulary — influences, moreover, which would have been thought the final manifestations of the romantic epoch, had not he found new beauty in its decadence. Schönberg's " Verklärte Nacht " and Delius's " Summer Night on the River " are both woven from the kind of harmony which was once thought to have reached its final limit in *Tristan*. The Schönberg work would have vindicated that opinion had we not known Delius; the Delius piece is not just an interesting freak or biological " sport ", like the Schönberg; it was alive when created and remains alive whenever performed. Before Delius

had been recognised by his own country he was accepted by the
Wagnerites of Germany, and we know that Wagner's was some
of the only music that gave young Delius extreme pleasure.
Yet where among his idyllic pieces is there any music that we
could mistake for part of the " Siegfried Idyll ", where any
writing to recall *Tristan?*

Again, though Delius lived in Paris before his marriage and
made his home near that city for the rest of his life, though he
had impressionist art around him and literature of that period
on his shelves, though his orchestral tints, his scrappets of errant
melody, together with other elements in his writing which are
difficult to isolate or define, may seem to have a purpose not
widely different from that of the impressionist composers of
France, where, even in the Verlaine settings, is there one work
to be mistaken for music of Debussy?

Delius is among the masters, then, because he was an artist
who surmounted his musical materials. It has been well said
that he was an artist first and a composer next, so that the child
is not wholly father of the man. This does not mean that he
would have held the same spell had he become writer, painter or
sculptor, but that we can hardly say of Delius, as of so many
composers, that in early days his problem was to *forge* a means
of musical expression. He greedily took just what music he
liked, beginning and continuing in an inveterate habit of improvisation. The process of natural selection from materials thus
acquired took its course without effort in obedience to his
primary desire to create and express. Improvisation was so easy
to him that he thought it as much a gift as ambidexterity; some
men were just born with it. Good coherent composition, as
distinct from a lavish spate of this natural gift, gave him as many
hours of hard work as forging a technique might have given to
another composer.

In an age when men glorified a being known to Wagner and
Nietzsche as " The Artist " (not a mere composer, writer or

dramatist!) Delius shared the individualist conception to a marked degree. The finished, triumphant artist was a conqueror who pleased himself first and compelled others to be pleased with him ; the growing artist was an adventurer of high courage and self-reliance (words which came from Delius's mouth in and out of season) who went his way and let the rest of mankind take or leave him. A period of adventure or battle is necessary to the making of such a being, and Delius had his inner and outer struggle. The inner one is the main subject of this study ; the outer one has been much exaggerated. Whereas Wagner's struggle involved drudgery, risk, and the kind of adventure which plays havoc with any man not blessed with Wagner's iron nerves, Delius's rebellion involved only risk, the exhilarating element in a fight ; most of the risk was on the not unenjoyable physical level, for he must have known that financial difficulty would have been merely temporary. At no period of his life does he seem to have suffered a long spell of soul-destroying worry, or to have been in dire straits to obtain the means of existence. Apart from the physical tragedy of his old age, troubles were entirely those of his musical vocation.

But the adventurous nature was always with him, even when his domestic life was settled and secure, and there is no composer whose early biography makes more romantic reading than that of Frederick Delius. Was he not handsome, a good athlete, charming of manner, liked by men who did not know him as an artist and by women who did not hope for him as a husband? Was he not a rebel and a wanderer at home, in Europe, in a romantic corner of the New World, a Bohemian in Paris in its famous days of bohemianism, a rebellious Nietzschean? Was he not a very Childe Harold in youth and, in his last years in the bath-chair among his flowers at Grez, was not the stricken figure also a striking figure? Did he not till the end stir the romantic emotions?

So does his music. Be it erotic, contemplative or as boister-ously jubilant as a pagan festival, it rarely fails to make us think that the world is ours to roam. Always, as we listen to Delius's best work, we are aware of a horizon and of a will moving towards the exploration of its beyond.

CHAPTER TWO

PARENTS AND HOME

THE horizon, the call to adventure, was in Delius from
early years. Seen against the stern government of his
home, or the Bradford outlook of the seventies and
eighties, his youthful escapades, such as running away from
home across the Ilkley Moors fully provisioned with sweets,
were not less daring than the wilful movements of his later years.

Were it not that his father's temperament and behaviour did
as much to make Fred as to unmake the elder son, Ernest, and
to have disunited the family generally, it would not be necessary
in a short biography to give a lengthy description of the composer's home and family. It happens, however, that Fred inherited his father's hardness, though noticed chiefly in his later
days and not exercised in the same directions. Some of Delius's
more uncritical admirers were annoyed when Eric Fenby, in
Delius as I Knew Him, exposed this side of the composer's
character.

Julius Delius, who has slipped into the list of martinet
fathers, was also a person of kind heart and lavish generosity.
His was not the public munificence which advertises a business
man ; one of his warehouse managers declared that " though
his family and business subordinates lived in fear of him, he
seemed to believe every hard-up story that came his way ".
Julius was of Prussian stock, his father having been made burgo-
master of Bielefeld in Westphalia for services under Blücher.
The composer's father came to Yorkshire in 1850 and set up
as a buyer and seller of Australian wool in the heyday of un-

8

restricted enterprise. He took out English naturalisation papers almost immediately. This commercial venture was as much a departure from family tradition as his son's insistence upon a musical career, for the Deliuses had been pastors or professional men of some kind in days before Bielefeld became the centre of a big Prussian linen industry.

Julius addressed his wife as " Madam ". With these courtly manners, and with Prussian fastidiousness of dress and toilet, which he imposed on the children, he received considerable surprise at the bluntness of speech, dress and manners among Bradford business men, whose mode of living and leisure tastes differed only in costliness from those of the workpeople. There was one interest, however, which he shared with his neighbours in a West Riding yet innocent of organised and commercialised sport — the making and patronage of music. He had chosen his wife from a music-loving family of Bielefeld into which Deliuses had previously married; yet even she, outliving Julius long enough to see Fred's musical triumph, persisted to the end of her life in maintaining her husband's opinion that a life dedicated to music was no life for a gentleman.

Elise Delius presented her husband with fourteen children, of whom two died in infancy. Frederick, or Fritz as he was called in the nursery, was the fourth child and second son, born January 29th 1862. The activities of the composer-to-be, the ordered life of the family, treats bestowed from above and forbidden treats discovered for himself — these are told with enjoyable detail in Clare Delius's life of her brother.

There was more good music to be heard in Bradford during Delius's childhood, if we reckon per square mile or per head of population, than in any other city of the United Kingdom. Before London had regular first-class concerts, Charles Hallé's orchestra could be heard regularly in Bradford, and when we note that among visiting musicians who played in the Delius household were Joachim and Piatti, one may doubt whether the boy could have heard better music elsewhere in England than in his own home. Concert programmes were still stuffed with the weaker kind of Victorian music, but Bradfordians, and the Deliuses especially, had tastes not yet acquired by a wider audience. They showed lavish hospitality to musicians, but could not conceive how a person of their class proposed to make music the expression of his whole life and being. Music was the best, most civilised, of spare-time occupations.

In fairness to Julius it must be emphasised that Fred's love of music was thoroughly encouraged. His gifts were recognised with approval, and schooldays had to pass before he showed to others than his father that those gifts were of genius. After all there were twelve Delius children, all more or less musical, Ernest being conspicuous for his share of that ability to improvise at the keyboard which Julius himself possessed, though unable to take part at sight in concerted music. Of the four sons, Fred was merely the most vigorous and attractive, the leader in childish mischief and make-believe, in sports and amateur theatricals, and the favourite with other members of the family, probably with his father. It seemed natural that he should also lead in the family music, and he was " brought down " to display his improvisation for the entertainment of visitors.

Many boys have shown as much natural ability, and too much importance should not be attached to the composer's own recollections of childhood, imparted to Heseltine and others. Old men's memories often play them false. No one will doubt that the more romantic pieces he heard — a Chopin waltz, the " Ride of the Valkyries " under Hallé, *Lohengrin* at Covent Garden — were among his most memorable experiences. They would have been so for most boys. But it is difficult to believe that, after only two hearings, he could play the Chopin waltz by memory. One has heard memory-playing by the unfledged only too often, and Chopin's harmonies are unusually subtle.

It is also difficult to accept the following : " His father's

passion for chamber music brought the quartet parties from
Manchester, Leeds and the neighbourhood to the house at
regular intervals. To his son, however, this surfeit of good
things became a little wearisome and developed in him a dis-
taste for chamber music which lasted many years " (Heseltine).
Clare Delius tells a different tale. After describing Fred's improvisation of programme-music for the other children, especially
when he had heard the travel yarns of a sailor lad whose company
he sought clandestinely, she adds : " Throughout his schooldays
his greatest joy was going to concerts. No matter how classical
they were, Fred was always lost in a trance of bliss ". It is
obvious that so highly musical a nature could be held by absolute
music, and not just by music with a literary or pictorial background such as attracts an unmusical boy.

    Delius could play simple things by ear at the age of seven,
when he began violin lessons with " Mr. Bauerkeller of the
Hallé orchestra, who came over from Manchester specially to
teach me. Later on I had another teacher, Mr. Haddock from
Leeds." These must have been good teachers ; one might
suppose that a harmony-loving nature like Fred's much preferred the keyboard, yet he became a fine violinist while neglect-
ing pianoforte study. He was praised by Joachim when, as a
boy of twelve, he deputised in a trio for the third professional
performer, who was ill. Pianoforte lessons began the following
year. Whoever taught him succeeded neither in forcing technical drills upon him, nor making him force them on himself
from a vision of their result. It took a hearing of Chopin's
" funeral march " sonata to do that, later on in his teens.
Instead of applying himself to technique, he spent tireless hours
at the piano, reading music and finding what it was made of,
whether or not he could name such things as chords and their
inversions. Recognition, not classification, is what matters to
the budding artist.

    In Bradford the boy's musical centre was his home, for during the years of his daily attendance at Bradford Grammar School there does not seem to have been much musical activity there, if any at all. Conditions in such schools are very different nowadays and the school at Bradford had the shrewdness to get subscriptions for a fine room, built in memory of its one-time pupil and furnished for music-making.

The International College, Spring Grove, Isleworth, Middlesex, was a boarding-school far enough removed from Bradford, in which city, however, it had a good name among the well-to-do. Its outlook was unusually liberal ; many a modern school is more Philistine. Despite the usual initial homesickness, Fred was sorry when he had to leave the place. Neither he nor his brother Max had shown particular brilliance in the main academic subjects. Fred did well only in geography, which appealed to the explorer in him, in French and in German. Spring Grove had music-rooms and good pianos — in 1877 ! Both violin and piano lessons were maintained, and Fred had a generously frequent exeat to play with an amateur orchestra in the neighbourhood, or to attend concerts and operas in London, accompanied by one of the masters with musical tastes. We are told that, after such a trip, he played through the programmes to his school friends, and that " any boy with any voice at all was pressed into service " so that young Delius could have a good time in improvising accompaniments, which we may suppose were luxuriant. He excelled in cricket as a true son of Yorkshire, and some horseplay with stumps injured him sufficiently to put him in sick quarters with a long convalescence. To the delight of his friends he spent most of the convalescent period in the music-room.

He left Spring Grove towards the end of 1879, and then shades of the prison house began to close; he was tethered firmly to the wool trade. Making no pose as an artistic youth in an uncongenial place, he was liked by his colleagues during business apprenticeship, and when later he chafed at the bit, he showed

nothing but sociability in office hours. In the evenings he had
the blessed relief of music-making. One of the managers suggested that Fred should be sent as an agent to Stroud where,
despite runs to hear London music, he followed his father's
wishes so conscientiously that he definitely " promoted the
interests " of Delius & Co., inducing Julius to let him go to
Chemnitz and learn the trade more fully.   If Stroud was pleasant
after Bradford warehouses, the Saxon city was heaven itself.
Among its attractions were the theatre, opera and concerts of a
music-loving nation, together with visits to Dresden, Berlin and
other musical centres. The interests of Delius & Co. receded,
and a vaguely worded report, praising social rather than commercial gifts, brought Fred to a wrathful Bradford. He must
have been a beloved and persuasive son, for the same year,
1881, sees him off to Scandinavia for a second chance. His chief
associates were to be " such figures in the textile world as Ibsen
and Gunnar Heiberg " ; in due course came the peremptory
telegram.

    After the scenery of Norway and Sweden, Fred felt that he
had tasted too much of escape to endure the commercial con-
gestion of Bradford ; and though for the first time we hear of
open defiance and disagreement, one commercially successful
stretch of the recent tour elicited sufficient forgiveness to send
Fred abroad once more, this time under observation. Regularly
and privately from Saint-Étienne, the great French textile centre,
reports went to Bradford, than which Lyons and Saint-Étienne
were even more repulsive to young Delius. They were not
merely without natural beauty ; they were almost without music.
Boredom made him take a trip to the Riviera which he was able
to prolong through a piece of luck at the Monte Carlo gaming
tables. The inevitable cable ended the French adventure, and
again Fred was tried in Scandinavia. After yet another, and
final, shift to Manchester, trouble reached its climactic brew.
Julius's anger had already blazed against his eldest son Ernest,

who decided not to darken the same hemisphere as Sir Anthony Absolute ; he betook himself to New Zealand in the hope that live wool would prove less stifling than dead wool. Fred was the next black sheep to have the folly and effrontery to declare that he could not continue in the all-swaddling wool. The irresistible force met the immovable object, and after the first impact a miserable atmosphere of parental queasiness and filial sullenness overflowed the rest of the household. Since his body could not escape Bradford, Fred let his mind wander in maps and travel books, and he spent his days in the library. The artist wanted his time in the wilderness but, being Delius, he wanted a sunny, lush wilderness ; whatever the clime to which he proposed escape, his father must be convinced that he was going on commercial enterprise.

By what chance he requested to be sent as an orange planter to Florida it is hard to discover. Persistence won his father to the idea. Julius genuinely loved Fred and, now that he had come of age, perhaps the prodigal son saw wisdom ; and as he did not see it along the lines intended by his father, that father knew of a former son of the Delius family who had taken his own path and done remarkably well as a wool merchant. Fred should be financed and, of course, tied to the land of his choice. If orange growing did not thrive, if his substance were wasted in riotous living, never should he return as a son. He could reap the harvest of folly with the husks mentioned in scripture.

In March 1884 Delius set sail from Liverpool.

CHAPTER THREE

ESCAPE AND FREEDOM

THE Solano Grove, an old Spanish plantation with a name as blessed as Mesopotamia in the ears of D. H. Lawrence, who proposed to found a Shelleyan pantisocracy there, would commend itself as a residential area only to those who would conceive the erection of a temple of salubrity in the swamps of Bengal. Delius cherished no dreams of solitary dedication to Nature with the capital letter. The Solano Grove meant escape from the irate telegram, yet Julius sent one of his business managers all those thousands of miles to report. That assurance might be doubly sure, he bought the estate outright as soon as report told him that his son was absorbed by music instead of oranges.

Big business in oranges [1] was never uppermost in Fred's plans though the fruit may have delighted him for a week or so. The St. John River was several miles wide, and the grove, a wide tract hemmed in by virgin forest, could be approached only from the river. Even for so roving a fancy as Fred's, the place was romantic enough, and for the first time he saw the luxuriance of tropical vegetation. He himself did not vegetate, though his only instrument was a violin. Later, on the most important day in his early life, he acquired a piano, and his father's envoy found him, six months after arrival as new master of the plantation, working hard day and night — at music, at the piano or at

---

[1] Delius always spoke of the Solano Grove as a " grapefruit farm ", though the fruit was known by the name " shaddock ". He once perplexed a friend of the present writer by saying, " Shaddock the size of footballs lay rotting beneath the trees when I arrived there ".

15

counterpoint exercises. The oranges and grapefruit lay rotting under the trees, and this prodigal waste (what is more romantic than cultivated land going wild ?), the alarm of snakes, the songs of the plantation negroes, the river, all amply filled his senses during the small stretches of leisure from study. Accounts of his alligator shooting at night, with punt and lantern, make thrilling reading, though when we hear that his best alligator " was no less than seven yards long ", we may wish to hear about the other alligator, unless the length of the alligator's whiskers is counted.

Impressions of Solano are permanently enshrined in " Appalachia ", wherein the composer recalls the negro song with the refrain : " Oh honey I am going down the river in the morning ". Delius was more interested in his people's songs than in their day-labour. Not quite the same as the spirituals whose harmonic roots are in Victorian mission hymn tunes, they had the same nostalgia and accordion accompaniment, of a type too sweet and easy for any but such unsophisticated outpourings. How Delius must have longed to supply his own accompaniments, as among school friends at Isleworth ! A piano seemed a necessity to his happiness ; its purchase caused the most fortunate expedition of his life — a large claim, but he would have supported it.

Thomas Ward, organist of the Jesuit church in Brooklyn, could direct the disciplines of musical study in a thoroughly musical way. Such a teacher is rare. He knows his classics but knows also that responsive humanity, not a congress of teachers, made them classics ; he sees them as supreme records of expression, their technical processes being fascinating means to greater ends. The scarcity of such teachers lies in the fact that they cannot be truly happy with a pupil who does not show the same sensitivity and enthusiasm. Their pupils may or may not become known to the public, but their own modesty prevents their caring for other reward than seeing high ideals in the younger generation. Often they have no creative ambitions and are unaware of their excellence as performers. That they form the backbone of our musical culture many a reader can witness, and the present writer has in mind two schoolmaster musicians of Ward's type, organists with interests beyond the organ loft, to whom he is indebted for their opening of the golden gates. The worth of a Ward cannot be known until one has passed from his direct supervision, and met the type of professional teacher who is useful only if one requires a taskmaster in some branch of examination study. Delius was to have experience of this change.

He took a trip down-river to Jacksonville, the nearest township, in hope of hiring an instrument. In the music shop he met Ward, whose church authorities had sent him south for a health cure. He was the older man by a decade, and though Delius came under his instruction for only six months, he became acquainted with music of such variety as is seen between Bach's organ and keyboard works, played at home in the shack or at Jacksonville Roman Catholic church, Berlioz's treatise on the orchestra, which rarely fails to stimulate the budding composer even if its technical details are out of date, and the study of counterpoint. Ward had the sense to see that counterpoint was the chief technical need of a pupil whose knowledge of harmony was as nearly a musical instinct as the recognition of melody. He thought Fred should learn from teachers of greater reputation. A letter went to Bradford requesting permission to study at the Leipzig Conservatory. Peremptory refusal made Delius plan to get there by his own means. He had scruples about selling the plantation bought with his father's money, and wondered how else he should find the means to begin earning elsewhere. Bolt from the blue, that is from the river, his brother Ernest appeared like Micawber. He had not been markedly successful as a New Zealand sheep farmer; could Fred just — ? He could. If Ernest took over the grove, the property would still be in the family and Fred's qualms laid to rest. The grove changed hands.

In August 1885, Delius for the last time went down the river to Jacksonville where Ward could obtain for him at least the small earnings of a newly arrived music teacher. These he eked by singing in the choir and playing the organ at a synagogue, the good rabbi thinking perhaps that his name was of Dutch or German-Jewish origin.[1] Whether he held that illusion or not, the rabbi added his testimonial to Ward's when, in reply to a newspaper advertisement, Delius applied later in the year for the post of music teacher to the daughters of one Professor Ruckert of Danville, Virginia. The successful applicant would receive no fees, but he would be lodged, boarded and well publicised in Danville. Such promises are not always kept, but Delius arrived in Danville with his last dollar to meet what he described as the goateed personification of Uncle Sam. The professor kept his promise and, in cockney parlance, did him proud, announcing him as the "celebrated Professor Delius" who had vacancies for one or two pupils in violin, pianoforte, harmony, counterpoint, etc. Those who think that Delius was unfamiliar with the academic disciplines may be discomfited in knowing that the young teacher had no difficulty in fulfilling the professor's testimony to his "versatility and eminence". His playing of the Mendelssohn Violin Concerto at the Roanoke Female College, deliciously described as "A finishing school for Young Women of the Baptist Denomination", brought him much social success, and led many of the wealthy tobacco planters of the locality to put their daughters under his instruction, some at the female college. Recollections of Delius by former Danville pupils attest that he was a person of engaging manners and a great favourite with the ladies.

That he prospered is shown by the fact that he soon made enough money to think of Leipzig. In a very short time he

[1] Some of the composer's friends claim Dutch ancestry for him; others stoutly deny it.

would have enough for the passage to Germany and at least a year's independence. Ward had emphasised the desirability of study at Leipzig, and since he owed so much to Ward, what might he not one day owe to the notables of Leipzig? Time answered that question — " Considerably less ". But there is more in Rome than the Vatican.

The gentlemen of Danville shook hands and the ladies sighed their farewells. The celebrated professor deserted them to become organist of a New York church, and the news — the first for a long time — percolated as far as Bradford. His parents had felt anxiety concerning Fred's silence, and this latest information made Julius declare any work to be less shameful than playing music for money. He would reconsider his refusal. Let the young fool have his fling and Leipzig. It would both fulfil and shatter the dreams, and perhaps he would then settle down to steady business life.

In June 1886 Delius sailed home ; thence almost immediately to Leipzig.

CHAPTER FOUR

LEIPZIG AND PARIS

D ELIUS'S chief instructors in Leipzig were of such
diverse excellence as Dr. J. Brahms, Prof. P. Tchaikovsky
and Kapellmeister R. Wagner, whose treatise *Die
Meistersinger* was soon followed by *Tristan*; never did pupil
more avidly absorb what they offered him. These mentors
exerted their influence in evening and late night sessions, but at
first Delius was almost as industrious with his matutinal teachers,
who included Hans Sitt the violinist and Carl Reinecke the
pianist. Under others he merely sat; they were pedestrians
and need not be catalogued. With Nikisch directing the opera,
Brahms and Tchaikovsky conducting their own works at the
Gewandhaus, and the Brodsky Quartet playing the last Beethoven
quartets, we may not wonder that " all his days and a good part
of his nights were spent in hearing music, playing music and
talking music ".

We should not pass by Delius's enthusiasm at Leipzig with
a few casual remarks merely because he showed such an insular
and personal technique, demanding from us a different attitude
from that given to the older classics or even the chief nineteenth-
century romantics. We used to swallow a legend that Delius
was like the romantic musician of the cinema, who takes the
honeymoon and writes the symphony, that he never needed to
bother his head with the music of previous masters, especially
the more architectonic masters of academic courses. The legend
seems based upon a few chance-remarks reported by visitors to
Grez, for instance, " Why do you play that stuff ? " — the stuff

being one of the Beethoven violin sonatas. In the first place Delius liked argument and leg-pulling ; in the second his *obiter dicta* (if not most of his *dicta*) are of little permanent value, and often need salt ; and is even the Kreutzer Sonata a work one wants to hear frequently ? Is it one vast spiritual experience right through, including the variations ? That certain Delius legends are non-sensical, old Leipzig friends could tell. How could they be true of a man who declared that his finest memories of that time were of Reinecke's Mozart playing and the chamber concerts of the Brodsky Quartet ?

If the meeting with Ward was the most fortunate event in Delius's early life, his interest in Norway was one of the most formative influences. He had begun to master the language during visits as commercial traveller. Completion of mastery continued in the company of Norwegian fellow-students who, in 1887, took him for a summer walking tour in a country which he continued to hold in particular affection. When Grieg arrived in Leipzig later in the year it was inevitable that they should introduce their hero to Delius, and before the season was over Grieg was able to hear the orchestral suite " Florida " performed by an orchestra of sixty. A beer hall was the auditorium and payment was in kind from a large and specially subscribed barrel. Since the ripening friendship with Grieg is of importance, no apology is made for including the tale of another performance — proposed. Grieg gave a Christmas Eve party, inviting Sinding, Halvorsen and Delius, each being required to bring a work for post-prandial performance and judgment. The party won the day, for neither performers nor critics were in a state to pronounce upon " Sleigh Ride " by F. Delius.

Julius did not fail to notice the exact date when the eighteen months' course at Leipzig was past — and what had Fred to *show* for it ? Did the father expect a diploma, or a cash prize, or a national decoration ? His son was required to return at once and take up his life-work in earnest ; it was still far from Julius's imagination that Fred's life-work had begun already. Grieg's magnanimity helped Delius over what might have been the last and highest hurdle. Julius, being *au fait* with music and musicians, held Grieg in the high esteem accorded that composer by Englishmen in general, and could not but be honoured by the composer's invitation to dinner at the Metropole. For the first time he was told by one whom he had no power to contradict that he did wrong in denying artistic freedom to his son. Grieg amazed him, but convinced him neither that music was a life for a gentleman, nor that it warranted the same allowance granted for continental study which, after all, might be regarded as a limited version of the eighteenth-century grand tour.

His allowance cut to subsistence standard, Fred had to consider in what place he could live upon his resources with the maximum musical return. Norway and Leipzig might have been chosen but for the fact that a bachelor establishment was maintained by his Uncle Theodore in Paris. Theodore Delius was one of the last examples of the mid-century dandy, having Julius's fastidiousness without the militarism. Being a perfect gentleman, and recognising in Fred a charming young man with a mind of his own, he not only supplemented the allowance but made no attempt (it would have been vulgar) to watch over his nephew's life and movements. The same elegance, courtesy, generosity and disdain of prying had made Uncle Theodore a favourite visitor to the children at Bradford.

Theodore saw his nephew set up modestly, though after a few months Delius moved to a more attractive flat at No. 33 Rue Decouedic on the Montparnasse fringe of the Latin Quarter. He did not plunge into Paris musical circles. From now on his life was dedicated to his work, and after the working morning or working day he had time for the interesting people, now regarded as a galaxy, who haunted the famous quarter's cafés. He knew neither that he would one day be revered, nor that they would be honoured by their own people. He knew that he could at last be himself.

CHAPTER FIVE

DELIUS AS THEY KNEW HIM

CERTAIN relatives and friends of the composer dislike
James Gunn's academy portrait of Delius in his last days.
Others find one of his noblest qualities not unfittingly
immortalised in the marmoreal features of a stricken and proud
artist, whose image has the stoic dignity of a Roman aristocrat.
This is the figure of Fenby's *Delius as I Knew Him*. For most
of us who were fortunate enough to see Delius in the flesh,
probably during the 1929 festival concerts at Queens Hall, this
frail figure, his litter surrounded with flowers as though his spirit
were already leaving the stricken body, was also " Delius as we
knew him ". Fenby's careful record, Gunn's masterly picture,
our own last sight of Delius — all these have the mark of tragedy
rather than mere pathos, and tragedy implies nobility, which
none would deny in Delius.

We should be wrong, however, to let this picture remain in
our minds while we examine his chief masterpieces. Delius as
we knew him must recede and give place to Delius as they,
especially she, knew him. Cosmopolitan Paris brought this
being to artistic manhood ; it also brought a perfect marriage
such as is rare among people of a proverbial temperament, a
comradeship to be recorded in musical history as having few
parallels. Delius's courtship and marriage, like Schumann's,
coincided with his making the first scores which would have
honourable place in a Delius festival proposed for this year.

There is no justification for regarding Delius as a pathetic
figure, or as a composer whose worth was more tardily recog-

nised than is usual. His characteristic work was produced at a later age than that of some composers, and popular favour took the usual number of subsequent years to follow. In many ways he was one of the most fortunate of artists. Until the dreadful stroke, the effects of which were fully disabling only during his last nine years (and after all he saw the three score and ten of the psalmist's span), he knew the joy of living more than have others. He sings more than they of the transience of beauty, of the sad, sweet landscapes of recollection, because he drank more than they of the earth's beauty and riches. Other English artists, using a different medium of expression, are felt to be like him in their evocation of mystical beauty and melancholy ; among them we recall Traherne, Vaughan the Silurist, Thompson of the *Seasons* and Tennyson in those poems Delius himself liked. Yet in Van Dieren's words, not to be accepted unreservedly, Delius " would sing of the return to healthy, pagan, assertive life. No monumentalism, like that of Bach, and no twilight dreams of religious meditation. No airs and graces like those of the eighteenth century. And no leonine heroics mixed with obtrusive joviality, such as the revolutionary fervour of a Beethoven had made achingly familiar. This in particular was the faded modernism which irritated him in his young days. He was eager to discard this load of memories that pinned music to forgotten ideals, and to the personalities of equally forgotten strife around them." Forgotten ideals ! As Mrs. Squeers might say of this whole passage : " There's richness for you ! " Van Dieren's dated juggling with " -isms " does, however, give a facet of the truth. Though Delius became a witness to the fact that the ideals despised are not likely to recede until art ceases to be great, though he is recognised as the autumnal glory of romantic music, though his materials are traceable to the first cadence into which crept a dominant seventh, or towards which one of the parts poised a suspension, nearly every critic found difficulty in grasping his means and purpose. Though many

"MR." THOMAS BEECHAM (1910)

were aware of genius in the music which dates from Paris days, and though there is hardly a composer more directly understandable to an English concert-goer to-day, we must learn how his utterance was new at one time, not just " romantic in its own day " as Stendhal declared all art to be.

Delius lived in the Latin Quarter from 1888 to 1896. Before then he had written, among other pieces, a setting of Hans Andersen's " Two Brown Eyes ", the orchestral suite " Florida ", a tone poem inspired by the Hiawatha story, a recitation with orchestra using a melodramatic verse by Ibsen, and the two pieces " Marche Caprice " and " Sleigh Ride ". Of what superior quality are even the first compositions of his change to Paris ! The first year alone saw the finishing of the five Norwegian songs, some of which — " Slumber Song ", " The Nightingale " and " Summer Eve " — if not all five, are favourites to-day. We have no opportunity to judge the manuscripts of a " Pastorale for Violin and Orchestra " and " Rhapsodic Variations for Orchestra ", since the composer destroyed sooner or later every work that he found unworthy of a place by his best.[1]

Marriage drew from Delius, as from Schumann, an access of creative activity proved by Heseltine's list, which will be found copied and completed in Appendix A. First are the " Seven Songs from the Norwegian " which contain the better-known setting of Ibsen's " Cradle Song ", and the settings of " Evening Voices ", " Little Venevil " and " Secret Love ", poems by his favourite Björnsen. Though the cycle from Tennyson's " Maud " includes lyrics more successfully put to music by others than by Delius in 1891, he followed it immediately with the magnificent Shelley lyrics, " Indian Love Song ", " Love's Philosophy " and " To the Queen of my Heart ". These ecstatic outpourings of his and Shelley's rapture have no finer rivals of their kind. Both the ardent voice parts and the accompaniments are of a direct

[1] One is indebted to Heseltine for the chronological list of works given at the end of his book. Nearly all information about Delius's production at this or that period is taken from Heseltine's list.

quality rarely used by Delius. In the next year he finished the three-act opera *Irmelin* to words of his own fashioning. The rest of his stay in Paris is worthily represented in the tone-poem " Over the Hills and Far Away ", the exquisite Verlaine songs, the orchestral variations now known in their " Appalachia " version (a revision of the original score), and the beginnings of *Koanga*.

Jelka Rosen [1] first saw her husband among the frequenters of an unpretentious café opposite her lodgings in Rue de la Grande Chaumière. The proprietress had no objections to credit, but liked her more impecunious and hand-to-mouth clients to leave some token which might be redeemed later. Thus the establishment had upon its walls at one time half a dozen Gauguins which would fetch fabulous sums to-day. The company of the *crémerie* did not, so far as we know, include other musicians than Delius, and though he knew and admired Ravel and Florent Schmitt, the former of whom made a piano transcription of the opera *Margot la Rouge*, and the other of *Irmelin* and *The Magic Fountain*, his friends were not normally any prominent members of Paris musical circles, which Delius seems to have avoided. The artistic and literary companions noted by the Norwegian lady artist, who was to become his comrade and wife until his death, were Gauguin, Strindberg, Mucha (a sculptor later honoured with the Legion decoration), the poet Leclerc and a Polish painter called Slivinsky. A measure of Jelka Rosen's love for her husband was her exchanging the natural ambition of an artist, whose work had appeared in the *salon* when she was a girl of seventeen, for life companionship with a musician.

Other men in the Paris circle achieved public recognition in future years, and it is more than likely that Fred met Paul Verlaine. Strindberg, however, was the composer's chosen companion on walks through the Luxembourg Gardens, the

---

[1] " Mrs. Delius was partly Jewish, as her mother was of the English branch of the Moscheles family." — May Harrison.

Jardin des Plantes (monkeys fascinated the dramatist), the Champs-Élysées and other pleasances. The accounts given by Heseltine and by Clare Delius may be consulted by those who seek interesting and amusing anecdotes of Strindberg's eccentricities — his abortive scientific inventions, and the practical jokes played by Delius and others of the fraternity to cure his belief in table-rapping.

In 1894 Theodore Delius died, leaving Fred a small legacy of unusual value at that particular stage in his career. One of the first purchases made from Uncle Theodore's bequest was a fine Gauguin, called " Nevermore " after Poe's verses " The Raven ". Gauguin, poorer than most struggling artists, cannot have expected the receipt of so generous a sum as £20. In later years, when the high tide of the German invasion overswept France almost to include Grez-sur-Loing, the village of Delius's final home, he and his wife took more trouble over the Gauguin than they did over any other single possession. Fortunately their exile to Orléans lasted only eighteen days, during which time the large cylinder with the rolled-up canvas had to be protected in a crowded cattle truck and on railway platforms crammed with refugees.

Delius did not buy his house and garden at Grez until late in 1899, so that his married years in Paris, interspersed with visits to Norway, Germany and England, are of considerable musical importance. The biographical events of this period are uneventful, but we must trace the passing years by music which culminated in the pieces selected for the first Delius concert to be given in the composer's native land. Among the works at that St. James's Hall concert, neither the five Danish songs nor the orchestral pieces " Over the Hills and Far Away " (used as overture), " The Dance goes on ", nor the " Legend " for violin and orchestra, are of the greatest interest, although some of them are firmly established in the repertory. But the choral and orchestral excerpts from operas tell us two facts : first that Delius cannot have given himself much unproductive leisure while in Paris, for three dramatic works are represented, and only those who have essayed this form know how much labour is involved ; secondly that his self-criticism was of an abnormally fierce type, even for an artist of his dimensions. Of the three-act opera *The Magic Fountain* we have heard nothing since ; no part of it was included in the St. James's Hall concert, but previously it had been translated, copied and accepted for production at the Weimar Opera House. The pleasure of witnessing one's work rarely comes to a musician in his thirties, and only a man of Delius's integrity could have withdrawn it at the eleventh hour because he had misgivings about its artistic worth.

The first dramatic work represented at the 1899 concert, by items from an orchestral suite, is Gunnar Heiberg's *Parliament*, a satire produced in Christiania with incidental music by the dramatist's friend Delius. The play ran for six weeks to packed houses, though feelings waxed stormily between two camps, one of which thought the satire to apply particularly to Norway, and the other considering the humour to be levelled entirely at professional politicians the world over. Delius was the special villain of the one party, since he had seen fit to make a point by shameless transformation of the Norwegian national anthem. A blank cartridge, fired at one performance, caused the composer's eviction from one hotel and his refuge in another ; the scandal had no official settlement until, after a special debate at the university, pronouncement was made that patriotic sentiments had been in no way violated by the musical jest.

Of more lasting worth were the other excerpts from choral and orchestral compositions intended for theatre or concert hall. *Koanga*, represented by the prelude to Act III and the choral writing and finale of Act I, seems to have been in these portions exactly the opera we have now heard ourselves. It was written between 1895 and 1897. How far it is an advance upon *The Magic Fountain*, one cannot say, since Delius suppressed the score which might tell us ; if, however, *The Magic Fountain* were withdrawn because it was felt to lack consistency, either in its musical quality or its dramatic movement, then *Koanga* must be much the better work, for it has survived while the one-act piece *Margot la Rouge,* composed at least five years afterwards, has remained unpublished and unsung. Just as the Shelley songs of 1891, or the Verlaine settings of 1895, are finer than some later songs from Delius's pen, so the beautiful legend of Palmyra and Koanga brought finer music from him than did the sordid Bohemian scenes of *Margot,* whose killings, jealousy and melodrama would have made more useful grist to an Italian mill of the *verismo* period. Probably the finest item in the 1899 programme was not from an opera, though written for baritone solo, chorus and orchestra. This was the Midnight Song of Zarathustra, which now forms the beautiful close of " A Mass of Life ". That it does so shows the truth of the opinion, which is neither laudatory nor pejorative, that Delius's approach and technique was substantially the same in 1898 as in 1905, or indeed 1925. Musically this composer, on his way from young man-hood to middle age, the hair just beginning to thin and recede from the forehead, is Delius as we knew him.

The 1899 concert marks the beginning of Delius's progress as far as gradual recognition by the musical public is concerned. Nobody in England knew what sort of stuff was about to be heard at the concert, and an evening devoted to one man's pro-duce was unusual if not unique. The audience received well both the man and his music, and the critics, with the conservatism that is on the whole a good characteristic of our tribe, recognised sincerity, genius and beauty, in parts if not in wholes. How could critics of the nineties fail to fish out the delicious word " bizarre ", so carefully nourished by Wilde to have a flavour near to that of " exquisite " ? There may seem little about those pieces nowadays to fan the faintest whiff of the nineties, but should we not have suspected, had we been called upon to judge at that

time, that the less abiding features of the music were comparable
with passing aesthetic expressions and perversions in other arts ?
Was not the mature Delius, the best Delius, a man of the nineties,
whose ideals of beauty had much in common with those of people
whose smaller size made them figures only in freakish and abortive
groups ? Did not even these movements do some good to greater
art ? And to the end of his life was not Delius's mode of living
such as the greater and more balanced aesthetes of the nineties
would have liked ?   Did not his taste in reading and pictures include prominently the typical writing and painting of that *fin de
siècle* ? The critics more nearly shared the enjoyment of the
audience in 1899 than they have done in the presence of new
music on many subsequent occasions. The *Musical Times* repre-
sentative, who held the most famous item to be " a setting . . .
of an incoherent poem called *Also sprach Zarathustra*," was neither
malicious nor foolish. That paper calls Nietzsche's work exactly
what it is, and its criticism of a different music from Wagner's, or
from the " Zarathustra " of Richard Strauss, which must have
become already known, was consistent with its policy towards
new music since — to encourage experiment and, when something new is hard to assimilate, to describe its features without
appraising them. Journals written for professional and by professional musicians rarely wax rapturous over a newcomer, and
it is well that they do not ; often the professional critic must
know that the tremendous enthusiasm of a concert crowd cannot
come entirely from delight in ephemeral appeal in the music,
nor from liking for the composer, nor from well-planned puffing
by agents or clique ; he must sometimes feel fairly sure that
genius is present, but he has seen clever men come and clever
men go, and his writing will be more cautious than the reporting
of newspapers which do not cater specifically for musicians.

   It is difficult to know why early press notices of Delius are
held to ridicule as obscurantists' attacks. What a pity so
many critics to-day become sciolists or, instead of listening

to works as works, are influenced by opinions broadcast by radio, by a composer's social standing or by his places of education and travel. The generation of critics who pronounced on the first Delius works to be heard in England more faithfully strove towards Saint-Beuve's critical ideal " *ériger en lois ses impressions personnelles* " than do many of the brotherhood to-day.

What could be sounder or fairer to a new composer than the following :

England ought to know something about one of the few composers of genius she has had the good fortune to possess . . . the bold harmonies and complex details disturbed one at first, but by the end of the concert one was convinced that these were not the bizarre affectations of a clever young man, but part of an original composer's great design. Mr. Delius's peculiar gift is the welding of apparently irreconcilable atoms into an exquisitely simple whole.

It is plain that other critics felt that much they heard at the 1899 concert did consist of " the bizarre affectations of a clever young man ", yet one of the least laudatory notices spoke of " the moving of waters, as it may be described, within the depth of the music far below the surface ", thereby showing the faithful recording of impressions shared even by modern listeners. Another writer, who found much of the music " discordant, harsh and uninviting ", had the sheer good sense to add :

He made it so with a definite purpose in view, and I can quite imagine that I might get to like those discords if I knew them better. That is what happened with Wagner's music. . . . I have no right to say to a composer : " You must not speak to me in that tone of voice " . . . for that tone may be part of the very individuality of the composer.

Why, then, did England forget Delius for eight years after the 1899 concert ? — if we are to judge by the fact that no work by him was played by any orchestra in this country until London heard the Piano Concerto in 1907 with approval and critical stirrings of conscience, expressing both approval and stirrings through its press notices ? To answer this question we must

forget an England of good gramophone recording and broadcasting, in which, though one composer may " get the start o'
the world " through favour with clique or society, though
another's work can be published, puffed and performed in the
very teeth of disapproval from professional musicians, yet no
new composer can say that he has *no* chance of a hearing, unless
his work lies in opera.   The great risks and expenses of production can be avoided in a broadcast performance, and one sometimes thinks that one's hearing of *Koanga* and *A Village Romeo
and Juliet* at home in a chair, with no light but that of a small
fire, is done in conditions which Delius himself would have
enjoyed.   Then, too, Delius's music, even under fine conductors, never sounds as it does with Beecham's direction ; and
modern conductors have the Beecham performances from which
to learn.   Between 1899 and 1907, there was no highly gifted
compatriot with the insight, the money or the influence to do
for Delius what Beecham did in the following decades.   Wood,
who did more for new composers than did other English conductors, began the infiltration of Delius into our programmes
by including the revised piano concerto in a promenade concert
of 1907.   Beecham came on the scene two years later.

The 1899 concert was a flash in the pan which can have had
no effect upon the spread of Delius performances in his native
country.   From the 1907 promenade concert, gradual recognition began at the usual rate for new composers before broadcasting days, being accelerated by Beecham's championship later
on.   The eight years, then, between 1899 and 1907, during
which Fred's birthdays passed from the thirty-seventh to the
forty-fifth, can be regarded from one point of view as the most
and only disappointing period in his career.   The man himself
was probably never happier, for during that period his mind
was conceiving and shaping those works in which we now find
the quintessence of his utterance.   Once the new campaign had
begun, in the last year of that period, with the promenade per-

formance of his piano concerto, we see from year to year the launching of such favourites as " Songs of Sunset ", " Brigg Fair ", " In a Summer Garden " and the first Dance Rhapsody. Still greater than these, those works for chorus and orchestra, " Sea Drift ", the " Mass of Life " and the opera *A Village Romeo and Juliet,* which are the very summit of Delius's achievement, were all composed during this hidden period.

CHAPTER SIX

GREZ-SUR-LOING

No shrewd French or German critic at the 1899 concert would have failed to see that Delius's materials, though eclectic, had neither Gallic nor Teutonic centre of gravity ; in the course of listening, what was obviously Nordic would show itself English. It is doubtful, however, if the fact would have been immediately recognisable by the average English concert-goer until the works of 1899 had been augmented by " Brigg Fair ", " On hearing the first Cuckoo in Spring " or " In a Summer Garden ". The extremely insular utterance of these works, written after Delius's settlement at Grez, has from that day to this held them in the greatest affection among the composer's countrymen.

What Londoner in 1909, hearing the last piece mentioned at its first performance, did not suppose the garden to have spread its sweetness towards an English river ? Yet who to-day, knowing the outline of the Delius legend, as most musical folk do, fails to associate this work of his prime with the garden at Grez ? Many have made the pilgrimage from Paris through the Bois in order to experience emotions they had previously known in Delius's music. But for his home there, or for some photograph seen in a book, article or concert programme, few pilgrims would have given heed to its mention by Stevenson, who haunted the village in days when other travellers stayed only in Fontainebleau or Barbizon.

Grez-sur-Loing, which " wantons idly in the summer air " as surely as does the euphony of its name, is described in *Essays of Travel*. The village roadway runs actually through the Norman church tower towards a long, low bridge. Delius's garden reaches to the river a little way downstream, but the garden of Stevenson's inn is close to the bridge on the other side. Nothing remains of the " romantic ruined castle ", though Delius's house was originally added to a feudal château, little of which is evident in the typical French country-house roofs and shuttered windows. Delius made his music, and his wife set up her studio, in fine large rooms which contained all the composer loved in small possessions — his books, his wife's pictures, his grand pianos, the Gauguin and other treasures. The storerooms outside were filled with the bounties of orchard and garden ; he kept a good cellar and, we are told, " a perfect cook ".

This lovely home was acquired almost immediately after the St. James's Hall concert. Lloyd Osbourne, who first met R. L. S. in Grez, and became his stepson, was a close friend of the composer. Since the first works to be finished in the new home were his finest creations, *A Village Romeo*, " Sea Drift " an " A Mass of Life ", Delius could forget his country's forgetfulness, and did not even cross the Rhine each time there was evidence that Germany remembered him. Continental musicians who believed in his genius secured enough performances of his work to keep a small flame alight, though " Paris ", the first orchestral piece from Grez, did not capture the city of its name so close at hand. It was played within a year of its composition under Hans Haym at Elberfeld, and the same conductor directed the first performance of " Appalachia " in its revised form. " Sea Drift " was chosen in 1906 for the music festival at Essen, and " Brigg Fair ", of all thoroughly English works, for a similar festival at Basle in the following year. But the climax of Delius's short-lived conquest of Germania was reached soon afterwards with the production of *A Village Romeo and Juliet* under Fritz Cassirer at Berlin, followed by Munich's performance of the " Mass of Life " (second part).

Ashamed though we may be of England during these years, once Beecham's energies made us recognise Delius, we accepted the whole Delius. Germany seems to have regarded him as a gifted modern composer, interesting because his harmony seemed the latest manifestation of post-*Tristan* technique, and because his largest conception was inspired by *Also sprach Zarathustra* at a time when Nietzsche had captured the spirit of young Germany. As England increasingly wanted Delius, and as, returning the compliment, his music became increasingly English, Germany's attention dwindled; there were always new composers to outmode the last, to provide material for argument and technical talk between concert and bed-time, and to swell the columns of German musical papers.

England began to mend her ways, or rather to begin afresh, in 1907, when the piano concerto was played in Queens Hall to an audience which happened to include Mr. Thomas Beecham, though the conductor responsible was, of course, Mr. Henry Wood, a friend to new composers throughout his long public life. Not content to include the concerto and then say: " Well, I have given him his innings ", Wood put down " Sea Drift " for the Sheffield Festival. By good fortune Fritz Cassirer, the conductor who had launched *A Village Romeo* in Berlin, was touring just at the time when Delius's music was enjoying this new penetration of his native land. Cassirer directed London's first hearing of " Appalachia ", and the performance had a reception so unrestrainedly enthusiastic that the composer was surprised and amused. He was called for by name to appear on the platform, and it can be safely said that this work, not one of Delius's supreme masterpieces, was the first wholly to capture English listeners and critics. A novelty it obviously was, as contemporary reviews show, but the epithet is usually applied to *jeux d'esprit*, and the novelty was made highly palatable by the honeyed English sweetness of the writing. While the audience could take delight in the orchestral and harmonic richness, neither was so advanced in this piece to seem unduly audacious.

Beecham's devotion to this music began at once, scarcely a concert under his guidance failing to include some Delius work. The size and determination of his campaign may be judged by stating what was performed on three evenings of three successive years :

1909 : First complete performance of " A Mass of Life ".
1910 : First English performance of *A Village Romeo and Juliet*.
1911 : London Concert entirely devoted to Delius's music, and including first performance of " Songs of Sunset " for soli, chorus and orchestra.

The quality of these concerts we are fortunately able to imagine, since to attend a Beecham concert to-day is to be almost sure of a superb performance of works by Mozart, Delius or both. Strange juxtaposition ? No, not for this particular conductor.

Sir Thomas's particular vein of verbal humour, his gratuitous pronunciamenti upon topics musical and otherwise, together with eccentricities of which he is probably as aware as we are, might lead the ignorant to imagine that caprice and superficiality invade his art. Our national temperament expects cricketer and M.F.H. to take sport seriously, and is suspicious of the integrity of judge, cleric or artist who does not maintain the so-called virtues of *gravitas* and *probitas* in play as in work. The walking and talking caricature of *gravitas* which elicits mirth almost before he has spoken, cannot rob Sir Thomas of the honour he holds, among the gravest critics, as a conductor less frequently guilty of unjustifiable licence in his readings than is any of his fraternity. (The present writer cannot bring himself to write " peers " since the death of Leslie Heward.) Beecham does not " stunt with the score ". When does he make a vulgar change of speed between contrasting themes and moods of a symphony, or rush a scherzo so that horns miss and strings blur their notes, or make a minuet into a waltz, or fail to play a slow movement without sentimentality or loss of rhythmic vitality while keeping it a genuinely slow movement ? A conductor with Beecham's uncanny sense of the exact initial tempo for piece and place, with his exacting standards of articulation, varying tone and orchestral balance, his consistently firm grasp of music passing and music coming, that never degenerates into regimentation of the players — such is the man for the fastidious and aristocratic Mozart ; such is also the man for Delius, also fastidious and aristocratic, the fluidity of whose music makes it a Tom Tiddler's ground for weaklings and charlatans of the profession.

Coming later on the scene, when England was ready for Delius's greatest music, Charles Kennedy Scott did for Delian choralism what Beecham did for the orchestral works, merely from high standards and ideals, and the ability to make the singers share them. Collaboration of the two musicians, as in the memorable last concert of the 1929 Delius Festival, made possible performances which have not yet been surpassed and, in view of the wretched standard of present-day singing, are likely to remain unsurpassed in our time.

But for the physical affliction of Delius's last years, we might conclude his biography at this point with a few rema s on his personal character ; for the Delius represented in the most frequently heard music is the recluse of Grez-sur-Loing, pantheist and Nietzschean ; a list of each year's works and of their public reception makes dull reading. The last of those specifically English nature poems — " Brigg Fair ", " On Hearing the first Cuckoo ", etc. — formed the suite called " North Country Sketches " ; it happened to be finished during the first year of the Great War, which catastrophe may fitly divide Delius's creative life at Grez and enable us to consider him as man and musician before, during and after the war years.

Despite the evacuation order, Grez-sur-Loing received

nothing at German hands worse than the noise of gunfire; but damage to Delius's house, especially the interior, was wantonly done by French officers. Any musician who has found himself dressed temporarily as a gentleman during national emergency must have wondered why wilful destruction and waste at such a time, though punishable in the ranks, is a time-honoured privilege and tradition among his gallant peers. Delius's experience of a universally accepted stupidity needs no commiseration. Wine, silver and other valuables eluded the occupants, having been elaborately hidden underground, and the composer's exile did not last three weeks. He was, as usual, fortunate. Few other Englishmen, and no other musicians and composers of England, escaped great privation and suffering, even when their physique prevented their enduring the horror and weariness of battle. Delius, having suffered almost nothing from the impact of war, not even a long spell of separation from friends, regarded it as an " outrageous interruption " of his work (Clare Delius). Annoyed at the havoc in his house, he almost immediately came to England. Did Delius know that his idol Nietzsche took a very different attitude to the Franco-Prussian war ? It does not matter that Nietzsche actually felt it his duty to join the army medical service in the battle area ; the contrast between Delius and Nietzsche would have been similar had the latter thought it his duty to suffer imprisonment, or ostracism, as a conscientious objector. The point to be emphasised is that some artists have a social conscience and others have not. Delius's at least gave him little trouble, a fact to be recognised in the nature of his musical tribute to " all young artists who sacrificed their lives during the war ". What a contrast between Delius's " Requiem " and Elgar's " For the Fallen " !

We are not concerned with the rival musical merits of the pieces. Beautiful parts do not make the whole " Requiem " a piece of first-rate Delius, whereas Elgar's tribute is one of his most moving compositions. But were the artistic values reversed, the Delius comparable with " Sea Drift " and the Elgar a paltry occasional piece, the texts and the approach to those texts would distinguish the two men. Elgar's noble voice has already expressed our common emotions after the latest folly and carnage, and has been used every year since its composition, whether in heavy or distant shadow of war ; for no other composer except Brahms and Fauré has left us what we crave and shall go on craving while death, suffering and bereavement on a vast scale continue to visit the world, and to unite us in sorrow. To supply such a need, Delius might as well have offered portions of the " Mass of Life ". We need not let our personal, religious or philosophic bias enter the argument ; " For the Fallen " has no more of Christian doctrine than has the " Requiem ", and no Nietzschean would contradict his beliefs by setting such lines as " They shall grow not old as we that are left grow old ", " They are known . . . as the stars are known to the night " or " At the going down of the sun and in the morning we will remember them ". With or without Elgar, but more powerfully with Elgar, the poet identifies himself with humanity in general and is lost in the suffering crowd. When Delius is at his greatest, as indeed in the finer parts of the 1920 work, the reverse process happens ; his potency is such that the listener is held as in a spell, and must temporarily identify himself with poet and composer, whatever their outlook. That is why a concert-goer on the night of October 27th could lose himself in the loveliness of " Therefore eat thy bread in gladness, and lift up thy heart and rejoice in thy wine, and take to thyself a woman whom thou lovest, and enjoy life ", without asking what on earth such senti- ments had to do with " all young artists who sacrificed their lives during the war ". But when the same concert-goer, travel- ling to business on the morning of October 28th, thought he would read the composer's explanation of the work played on the previous night, his reactions to the following verbiage would have made an interesting study :

FRONT OF DELIUS'S HOUSE AT GREZ-SUR-LOING

DELIUS'S HOUSE AND GARDEN AT GREZ-SUR-LOING

It is not a religious work. Its underlying belief is that of a pantheism that insists on the reality of life. It preaches that human life
is like a day in the existence of the world, subject to the great laws of
All-Being. . . . Independence and self-reliance are the marks of a
man who is great and free. He will look forward to his death with
high courage in his soul, in proud solitude, in harmony with nature
and the ever-recurrent, sonorous rhythm of life and death.

The passage should be perused by all who talk of Delius as more
intellectual than most great artists. It is not required of a great
artist that he possess or develop intellect, provided he is intelligent in his art. Delius was more intelligent than most of us,
even outside his art, but he had so large a measure of artistic
egocentricity that he developed blind spots in his intelligence.
He thought himself the enemy of religious faith, but was himself
the slave of a self-concocted religion more bigoted than the most
ultramontane forms of catholicism or the most Calvinistic forms
of protestantism. His reading, if widespread, was not intel-
lectually wide. He read where he was sure to find what he
liked, where his own nature and mode of life was flattered. That
is the artist's mentality, not the impartial, broad-searching nature
that makes a philosopher.

Delius's blind spots—for nothing about the man can be called
a weakness—gave him a certain attitude towards the rest of mankind that made him assume it to be in anybody's power to lead
as free, as independent and as egocentric a life as he did. It does
not seem to have occurred to him that birth, money, physical
strength, nervous stamina, the devotion of wife and servants,
the absence of children from the household, had any part in
shaping circumstances. Apparently, to quote his notes on the
" Requiem ", any artist could have ideal conditions of work
through the sheer cultivation of " independence and self-
reliance ".

Reverses of fortune, the responsibilities of family and children,
or the need to do other work than composing, and thereby to

D

know more about other people — these things do not necessarily make any difference to the art of a supreme genius, though they make a difference in his personal character which most men hold to be an improvement. Did Bach's large family, his regular duties at church and school, alter the character of his music? Were Wagner's ordeals in Dresden, Riga, Paris, Bayreuth, essential in the making of Wagner? And is there, then, any quality missing in the work of a composer who can pursue his art in ideal conditions? One repeats — not necessarily.

Genius must shape and deliver its conceptions as the hen must deposit her eggs, though it detest the labour. But the minor artist, unless endowed with unusual strength, is likely to find his work deteriorating with the advent of ideal conditions and material good fortune. There is so much more than a garret-floor to pace when invention fails. He writes less, loses faith in the value of his work, is for ever playing or hearing the work of greater men, is distracted by the beauty of his surroundings and becomes dilettante in other matters than music. Often he becomes an excellent critic, for his own experiences have enhanced his insight into other men's music. Delius was not of this category. To say that genius is only an infinite capacity for taking pains not only errs in the " only ", but puts cart before horse. With the gift of supreme genius nature bestows enough egocentricity to compel taking of pains, concentration upon work in progress and the uncanny postponement of physical or nervous breakdown until the final bar-line is drawn. Thus neither Wagner's overwhelming worries on the one hand nor Delius's pleasance on the other impinged upon that egocentricity which is allotted for the safeguarding of artistic creation.

Had one dealt only with music it would have been as unnecessary to mention Delius's development of egocentricity beyond the necessities of genius as, in a discussion of the music-dramas, to mention Wagner's caddishness towards women or his cadging from friends. The fault does not seem to have hurt

those who lived with Delius, but it must be attributed to the fact
that no other composer has enjoyed, for at least thirty of his
most important years, so large a share of all that one supposes
an artist to desire. He could take for granted the devotion of
others — his wife, relatives, friends and servants, for he retained
the personal charm of earlier days, however often he chose to
hide it under intolerance or sarcasm. A fine old lady who had
retired from the Milan opera sat next to the present writer at a
concert of the 1929 festival. She had known Delius sufficiently
well to have visited him, and in those days, before the publication of Fenby's book, one was anxious to know something about
the composer's personality. She said : " Oh he is English, very
English, and hard as iron. But he makes his most hard remarks
with such a charming smile. He is as approachable as a child if
you are sincere, and he likes people who are not afraid to answer
him with contradiction."

The two statements made above — that Delius was approachable as a child, and liked those with the courage of their convic-
tions — are excellently illustrated in his relationships with the two
most important people, other than Delius and his wife, to be
connected with the house at Grez. Heseltine was the schoolboy
whose sincerity found Delius as approachable as a child, and
Fenby the young man from Yorkshire who was not afraid of
answering with contradiction. This does not mean that sparks
never flew. To expect no sign of irritation in a hot religious
argument from a stricken man approaching his seventieth year
(Delius was sixty-five when Fenby offered his services as amanuensis) is to expect candidature for canonisation. Artists and
idealists of any age, though usually unorthodox, hold their con-
victions fiercely.

CHAPTER SEVEN

THE CLOSING YEARS

ONCE surrounded by the home and its contents at Grez, with things that were so much a projection of himself, with a wife who believed as ardently as he in Nietzsche's advice to artists and who was happy in ministering and directing for him, he was always anxious to get back to Grez, even after the shortest absence. His few friends might visit him from time to time, but all were artists or " characters " ; he had no use for " simple, homely folk ", would not talk with villagers nor allow workmen near him. He scorned " the mob and the herd ". Some people may say : " Happy he who has the means to do so"; others, including most of the great musicians, from Bach and Beethoven down to Elgar, would say : " Unhappy and incomplete he who seeks to do so ". This is not a matter for biographer's approval or censure, yet one must acknowledge that, had Delius died in full health, we should have known less of the man and of his workings as an artist, since this man, who was no more afraid to reveal characteristics in himself which others could " like or lump " than he was to pass rough-shod over opinions which others cherished, kept himself away from most other musicians whose natures and tastes were unlike his own. No holiday away from Grez was a busman's holiday. His illness brought Fenby, and it brought pilgrims to Grez. From them we know most about Delius the man.

In 1911 began Delius's remarkable letters to Philip Heseltine, so that we are able to know much about the composer's opinions, of his attitude to men and things, during the period previous to

that covered by Fenby's *Delius as I Knew Him*. Few artists fail
to derive pleasure from letters of young people in their first
enthusiasm for the great one's work ; however adolescent the
expressions, or the unformed critical powers implicit within the
lines, they give assurance that the rising generation will keep the
works alive. Replies to such letters, or words spoken at eagerly
sought interviews, usually temper graciousness with the suggestion that the great one has a very full life — " Yes, do write
to me later on, and be assured that I shall take interest in your
progress, even though I may not find time to answer you ".
But to young Heseltine Delius wrote more letters during the
two decades of their friendship than he did to relatives and
friends of his own generation. Moreover he took care to preserve
Phil's letters, and their writer must have been more to him than
another highly intelligent and hypersensitive schoolboy. (Delius
was kind, both in material assistance and advice, to any struggling artist who showed talent. But if there was no ability, he
took the Nietzschean attitude of no pity or sympathy ; letters
were unanswered, or the reply was tart and final.)

Heseltine wrote to Delius from Eton. Their mutual correspondence continued till Heseltine's death, becoming less frequent
only when the younger man's visits to Grez made letters unnecessary or when, as he grew older, he felt less need to unburden
his hopes and aspirations to a man whom he knew to be not the
sole repository of truth or balanced opinion. His parents were
more indulgent than Delius's had been, but they intended him to
go up to Oxford and then to enter the civil service. Delius went
to the trouble of persuading them not to force the boy into
uncongenial occupations, since there was no financial urgency
to prevent his following the process of trial and error that
makes an artist. In Heseltine, Delius saw a youngster facing
the hurdles he had taken himself, though what this young man
wanted was injections of ruthless determination, of Delian
egotism.

I think the most stupid thing one can do is to spend one's life doing something one hates. . . . I do not believe in sacrificing the big things of life to any one or anything. Children always exaggerate the duty they have to their parents. Parents very seldom sacrifice anything for their children. In your case your mother has certainly not, since she married again. . . . I was in exactly the same position as you are when I was your age and had a considerably harder fight to get what I wanted. I chucked up everything and went to America.

That Delius was unable to cure Heseltine of his lack of ruthlessness or of those moods wherein he lost faith in his abilities we know from the fact the shy Heseltine became hidden under the rip-roaring Peter Warlock; the only reason friends could find for his suicide at the age of thirty-five was conviction that his artistic powers were spent. Those who dislike autocratic and ruthless natures like that of Delius, which would have expressed no disapproval of Wagner's commandeering of another man's money or wife, must at least remember that he held the opinions sincerely. He was kind where and when he thought kindness justified, and cruel towards anything, men or opinions, which he would have destroyed.

There are contradictory opinions in the letters to Heseltine :

One's talent develops like muscles that you are constantly using and training. Trust more in hard work than in inspiration.

and :

You know my opinion of contemporary music. For me music is very simple ; it is the expression of a poetic and emotional nature. Most musicians by the time that they are able to express themselves manage to get rid of most of their poetry and all their emotions. The dross of Technic has killed it ; or they seize upon one little original streak, and it forthwith develops into an intolerable mannerism — Debussy and Ravel.

Strange words from Delius, whose " mannerisms stand out a mile " !

I think it absurd that your music teacher gives you finger exercises. I would simply tell him that you did not come to Cologne for that purpose. If I were you I should go to the best theorist in Cologne and learn what you can from him ; as a critic and writer, it may be of some service to you — as a composer, none whatever. I do not believe in any music constructed knowingly on any harmonic scheme. Systems are put together from the compositions of inspired musicians. I don't believe in learning harmony and counterpoint.

No ; nor in learning to play the piano decently. Those who heard him improvise at the piano (a musician of the writer's acquaintance called it " the evening slide ") knew very well that, for all his natural harmonic gifts, his love of sonorities, his sense of climax, his sure grasp of *emotional* form — no doubt the most important gift or acquisition of a composer — his long fingers were clumsy and undisciplined. Because he could not play simple parts and figurations, and because every note he wrote was put to test at the keyboard, his inner parts, especially in string writing, had not that interest of progression which makes Elgar's scores the delight of orchestral players.

Learning kills instinct. You can't teach a young musician how to compose any more than you can teach a plant how to grow, but you can guide him a little by putting a stick in here and a stick in there. Composition as taught by our academies is a farce. Where are the composers they produce ? . . . They give us the flat beer of their teacher, but watered down. . . . Never believe the saying that one must hear music many times to appreciate it. It is utter nonsense ; the last resort of the incompetent ; the amateur musician is better without a knowledge of the science of music.

N.B.—One may ask of what use, without a full grasp of musical science, Fenby would have been to Delius, but the old heretic insisted that he would have been " of no use as an amanuensis if he had not been practically self-taught ".

Had it not been that there were great opportunities for hearing music and talking music, and that I met Grieg, my studies at Leipzig were a waste of time. As far as my composing was concerned, Ward's counterpoint lessons were the only lessons from which I derived any benefit. Towards the end of my course with him — and he made me

work like a nigger — he showed wonderful insight in helping me to
find out just how much in the way of traditional technique would be
useful to me. And there wasn't much. A sense of flow is the main
thing, and it doesn't matter how you do it so long as you master it.

With the last sentence most good counterpoint teachers would
agree.

Heseltine was one of the most frequent and regular visitors
to Grez, though we read of Delius's anger at some of his rowdy
companions. At Moncourt, along a lane just outside Grez, lived
" Old Joe ", Heseltine's eccentric uncle, who used to come into
Delius's neighbourhood on a tricycle from which painting
apparatus was hung. During the war " Old Joe Heseltine "
put about the story that Delius and the German servants were
spies ; diplomatic relations between the households were broken,
but sufficiently repaired later on for old Delius to be wheeled to
Moncourt in his bath-chair.

Heseltine grew up with a full knowledge of Delius's limitations, and even passed through a period of complete reaction
against his music, reserving full admiration only for a few works,
including " Sea Drift ", *A Village Romeo and Juliet*, " Brigg
Fair " and " Appalachia ". The judgment seems a sound one,
except in the inclusion of " Appalachia " which, for all the beauty
of some presentations of the rather banal plantation song, contains much " early Delius ". When Heseltine first met Fenby,
he was glad to have someone at Grez who could talk of the
polyphonic glories, the masses and madrigals, the modern works
which owed their beauty to a very un-Delian approach (Elgar's
" Introduction and Allegro " and Bartok's quartets for instance)
and the works of Viennese masters for which Delius had no
time. One courted scorn or grim silence if one expressed admiration for any music, ancient or modern, of the type called scholarly.
" He had as much use for monks, priests and nuns, as he had for
their music, and I had no patience with Fred's eternal tiltings
at Christianity." The old man admired Elgar's " Falstaff ",

and had unbounded admiration for Verdi's opera on that theme, but was disgusted at " Gerontius " and the oratorio composers in general.

If some space is given to comments on Heseltine's character, it is because, in diagnosing that character wrongly, Delius revealed much of his own outlook. No scholar's editions of ayres, madrigals, string fantasias and other treasures, no researches of Heseltine's thoroughness, have revealed more surely that their editor felt the music to be as living as that which might have welled from his own heart. In Irish phraseology, we may say that Heseltine revived nothing that was not already alive ; his critical writing was none the less scholarly because its enthusiasm made it enjoyable to read. Of this Delius was aware, though he did not like the music described in Phil's articles. He wrote to him in appreciation of *The Sackbut* and *Milo*, saying that musical journals were full of dead matter. Despite his reaction from Delian inebriation, Heseltine did noble work of liaison and propaganda, especially for the Delius Festival of 1929, but he rightly disregarded Delius's advice that he should push one talent to the exclusion of any other " . . . concentrate ; do not diffuse your energies in so many things ". Heseltine's greatness lay in his wide interests. England had not known such a song-writer since Dowland, nor can contemporary criticism show an abler and more attractive pen.

The first signs of Delius's dread paralysis became apparent in the middle nineteen-twenties. He visited London to see the production of Flecker's *Hassan, or the Golden Journey to Samarkand* at His Majesty's Theatre in September 1923, though he had written the incidental music to this poetic drama in 1920. Soon after this, his sister noticed " a curious change which filled me with alarm ". The inertia and listlessness which she says was creeping over him was only physical.[1] Two years later, Clare

---

[1] Some friends saw him at Rapallo in 1923 and 1924, and were surprised at the sudden change in his appearance. His wife carried a stool, on which he sat and rested even during short walks.

saw him at Oeyenhausen, where he was taking a cure for what
was regarded as a temporary lameness. He was in a bath-chair,
and had come to look like James Gunn's death-like portrait of
him. By the end of another year he could not walk or play the
piano; his limbs needed constant massage and went cold and numb.
Then his eyes became misty, and faded to complete blindness.

The young Yorkshire musician, Eric Fenby, offered to
become Delius's " hands and eyes " in the summer of 1928.
By that time Delius's wife had ordered a routine in the Grez
household that centred round the needs of the stricken composer. He was wheeled into the garden or along the lanes to
Moncourt or Fontainebleau, or taken in his chair set on a flat-
bottomed boat for short spells on the river. He wanted verbal
descriptions of everything before his sightless eyes, and loved
to feel the sudden warmth of the sun as it emerged from cloud.
At regular hours each day his wife, or others employed for the
purpose, read to him in German, English or Norwegian (French
he disliked); he had to be acquainted with the contents of *World
Radio* so that he could select programmes; he also listened to
the gramophone. He took special delight in visits of his
bohemian friends and of the few English musicians with whom
he was in sympathy — Howard Jones, Balfour Gardiner, Roger
Quilter, Norman O'Neill, Percy Grainger, sometimes Sir Thomas
Beecham and on one occasion Elgar.

Fenby's account of the conversation between Delius and
Elgar reflects the superb wisdom of the second giant of
English music. Delius had not known Elgar well until that
visit, though it lasted but a few hours. " My music will not
interest you, Delius; you are too much of a poet for a workman
like me." To this Delius expressed admiration for the " Introduction and Allegro for Strings " and for " Falstaff ", but said
he thought it a pity Elgar should waste energy in writing " those
long-winded oratorios, though you are not as bad as Parry, who
would have set the whole Bible to music had he lived long

enough ! " " That ", said Elgar, " is the penalty of my English environment." They talked about people they both knew, about what would grow in Elgar's garden and what would grow in Delius's, and what would not grow ; they talked about books and found they had many common favourites. Elgar " was as excited as a schoolboy about his first trip by air and insisted that, should I come to England again, I must travel by air ". As on all such occasions, champagne came forth. To the end, Delius would not forgo the pleasures of the table, being as proud of his cellar as of his music. " So long as I can enjoy the taste of my food and drink, and hear the sound of my music, I want to live. Not being able to see does not bother me. I have my imagination. Besides, I have seen the best of the earth and done everything that is worth doing ; I am content. I have had a wonderful life."

A further source of pleasure to Delius were the visits of such players as Beatrice and May Harrison, Lionel Tertis and, of course, Heseltine. Tertis came to play his arrangement for viola of Delius's second violin sonata, and May Harrison to play Fenby's score of the dictated third sonata. Another visitor was the 'cellist Barjansky, an odd sort of person, though he gave Delius much pleasure in his performance of the 'cello sonata and concerto, and the composer congratulated Fenby upon his accompaniment. This approval was sorely needed by Fenby, who was unable to take down at the speed of a stenographer something " drawled in a loud monotone that was little more than the crudest extension of speech ". Obviously the old man *heard* melodies which he thought he was humming or singing. At first he was irritated and disappointed when Fenby could not do the impossible. No doubt he thought him a " theoretical musician ", who wanted a recital of technical terms.

Mrs. Delius piloted the two men so that Fenby marvellously accomplished his task with a success beyond his hopes. As a Yorkshireman, he was *persona grata*, especially when they talked cricket or followed the test matches with the concentration and excitement of schoolboys. Jelka told Fenby to show another Yorkshire trait, and to stand up to Delius with a doggedness equal to his. So, when asked to take out and play from the MS. of " A Poem of Life and Love " and to give his opinion, Fenby dared what no man had dared before. He called it what it was — patchy and inferior. " My first unfavourable comment electrified him ", but in the end he said : " Select all the good material, develop it, and make a piece out of it. Take your time : never hurry in your work whatever you do. Avoid all fillings and meaningless passage-work." This task was a test of Fenby's insight. He passed with such flying colours that Delius said : " I can work with you. You are a natural musician. You have got the sense of my ideas in an almost uncanny way."

Some stuff from this manuscript was employed in a compact and attractive little work, which has stayed in the repertory, namely " A Song of Summer ", first played by Sir Henry Wood at a promenade concert. Neither " Cynara " for baritone and orchestra, nor " A Late Lark ", for tenor and orchestra,[1] nor any of the revisions of scores made ready for the 1929 Delius Festival, compares in quality with the few superb works written by dictation, with plenty of time for the process, after the excitement of the festival was over.

At first Delius thought that he would not survive a voyage to England, but he was persuaded to attend the festival by Sir Thomas Beecham, who arrived in Grez to plead with him. Such playing and singing of Delius's master works had not been heard before the festival concerts in the Queens Hall and Aeolian Hall in October 1929, and such performances have not been heard since. Those who were present can testify that never has music cast so uncanny a spell over an audience as it did on the last night of the festival, when the Philharmonic Choir and

[1] Though both of these were completed previously.

Beecham's carefully selected orchestra performed the " Mass of Life ". As the last word, " eternity ", echoed and died, it seemed that the music had no point which could be precisely considered its finishing mark. A tense silence followed the last audible sounds ; Beecham and the players did not move. Then began the applause and cheering, such as is not heard even in the football-match atmosphere of the last night of a promenade season. It is conventional to speak of so-many-minutes' applause, but if one goes strictly by the clock, a minute's applause seems tremendous. The first cheers and noise, after the silence was broken, lasted a full ten minutes, and all eyes turned to the balcony where Delius lay on his litter surrounded by flowers. For the first time, and the last, his compatriots heard his voice in public. Slowly but clearly he uttered a few sentences of thanks for his reception and for the performance, adding : " This festival has been the time of my life ". In a speech from the rostrum, Beecham declared that we " could give next week another festival of works which have not been included in these concerts. From his workshop, Delius has produced no fewer than two hundred works." This would mean little unless one remembered that Delius wrote few miniatures or trifles. In the streets, as the composer was wheeled to and from Queens Hall, rooms having been taken for the festival at the Langham Hotel just opposite, the musical public cheered him and held up traffic during his passing.

Earlier in the year, Delius had received news that he was to be made a Companion of Honour ; his was not a nature to accept public honours, for he held too many of their holders in contempt. But he accepted, as Elgar accepted, a distinction conferred upon music in a country which puts artists among the also-rans, after it has decorated the names of industrialists, financiers and civil or military officers. Delius was aged sixty-eight, but his country had yet another laurel to offer him by way of belated recognition of his genius. This—the Freedom of the

City of Bradford—gave him even more pleasure than the King's honour, especially since Bradford sent a deputation of its leading citizens to Grez with the illuminated scroll, and the old man (this was three years after the festival) was able to hear the names of other enrolled Freemen of the City, to talk about the moors and cricket, and to indulge in pleasantries about his escape from the wool business.

Fenby had a well-earned rest during the festival, though he heard some of the concerts. The atmosphere of the Grez house and the actual work of transcription were enough to tax the nerves of a less sensitive soul than he. " There was nothing of the sickly, morbid, blind composer as known by popular fiction, but a man with a heart like a lion and a spirit as untamable as it was stern. I have seen his expression suddenly lose its life and set as hard as stone, for no other reason than that the soup had not been sufficiently salted in the cooking. . . . This sternness was never far from him. It embarrassed the kindly Americans who had known him . . . and it terrified children. All too frequently there were periods when nobody came near the house for months on end, and I have gone as long as five months without speaking to a soul outside the household. . . . Delius's constant changeableness was the most difficult thing with which I had to contend."

The most wonderful results of Fenby's work with Delius were the pieces produced between the 1929 festival and Delius's death. The " Idyll " to Whitman's " Once I passed through a populous City ", for soprano, baritone and orchestra, took its opening music from the more inspired parts of *Margot la Rouge*, the unpublished one-act opera which he had written in 1902, when he wanted the money offered for a prize competition. The " Idyll " was performed at the 1933 promenade season, Dora Labette and Roy Henderson being the soloists. A lovely little piece for small orchestra, the prelude " Irmelin ", was a source of pleasure and surprise to the orchestral players when

Beecham used it as an *entr'acte* at the Covent Garden revival of *Koanga*. The full list of works composed in these last years may be seen elsewhere, but pride of place must go to the magnificent " Songs of Farewell ". Delius was anxious that Beecham should launch them, but a visit to Grez by Mrs. Samuel Courtauld secured their first performance at a Courtauld-Sargent Concert in 1932. Fenby says, " I was able to wire Delius that the new work had turned out well ".

It is hard, despite Fenby's careful account of the method by which Delius and he worked together, to know how the work was done in the time — the very short time — which could be given to it each day. The phenomenon baffled a hypnotist called Erskine, a Scot who actually succeeded in restoring the old man to some control of his limbs. Erskine was certain that much of the liaison could be explained only by telepathy. Fenby was allowed to leave Grez in 1933, to be sent for " if needed ". He felt sure that it was not for musical dictation that he would be summoned. Early in 1934, letters from Mrs. Delius said that Fred had been extremely ill, was more emaciated, and so racked with pain, which came in agonising spasms, that he could bear no noise, even of passing motors, and had to be doped with soporifics in order to get any rest. One can imagine the difficulty of nursing Delius, after the Nemours doctor had prescribed a strict and plain diet. To crown all, Jelka herself fell ill and had to arrange for an operation at Fontainebleau in May. Fenby could not come when she first appealed to him, but there followed letters from neighbours in Grez to Fenby, telling him that Jelka's illness was of a more serious nature than she had disclosed, and that, even if she survived the operation, she would be an invalid for the rest of her life.

Though Delius welcomed Fenby with tears such as his amanuensis and friend had never seen before, and though he was made to believe that his wife's illness would soon be put right, his condition deteriorated rapidly. He endured bravely, and Fenby tried to interest him by accounts of the recordings that Beecham was making for the Delius Society, and by reading to him from books of the kind he liked — *Huckleberry Finn*, and Edgar Wallace's thrillers. Within a short time of Fenby's arrival the anodyne made Delius unable to retain his food. He could not stay comfortably in one position for any length of time. More and more frequently morphia was injected, for the pain as each dose wore off became insufferable.

Jelka Delius came out of hospital before recovery from the operation, though it had been successful, and was in the house when Delius died, on June 10th. The body was buried without any form of religious service in the cemetery at Grez, but it was asserted that Delius had expressed a wish that his remains should lie in English soil, in a village churchyard of the south country, the soft rich landscape of which his music speaks. Some of his relatives and friends doubt the truth of this statement and declare that Delius wished to be buried either at Grez or in Yorkshire. However, through the agency of Beatrice and May Harrison, who lived at Oxted in Surrey, arrangements were made with the Vicar of Limpsfield, a near-by village, that Delius's body should be re-interred in the churchyard. Limpsfield lies among trees under the slopes of the downs, and the church is a small and beautiful Early English one built of chalkstone.

Delius's body was laid in English soil on May 24th 1935. Musicians came from all over England to pay their respects, and Beecham gathered together a small orchestra to play Delius's music at a service held in the church. While making the journey to and from England for this ceremony, Jelka Delius caught a chill which developed into pneumonia; she died soon afterwards, having survived the husband to whom her whole being was dedicated by almost a year. In his speech at the graveside, Sir Thomas Beecham, who had more right than anyone to pay such tribute, used the words which may best conclude this

DELIUS'S STUDY AT GREZ-SUR-LOING

THE RIVER LOING AT GREZ

account of Delius's life. " The most precious part of this man is the immortal part — his spirit as revealed in his work : and in whatever sphere that spirit is, I should like our greetings to pass beyond the confines of this earthly sphere, and let him know that we are here, not in a spirit of vain regret, but rather in a spirit of rejoicing that his work is with us and will remain with us for evermore."

PART TWO

A CRITICAL APPRECIATION
OF DELIUS'S MUSIC

CHAPTER EIGHT

DELIUS AND NIETZSCHE[1]

THOUGH from early manhood Delius read and re-read some of the prose-poems of Nietzsche, he was far from being the convert to Nietzschean philosophy which he thought himself to be, and we do not insult his specifically artistic temperament by declaring that he had not the speculative mentality of a clever schoolboy. Nietzsche himself, once attacked as a philosopher, is now admired chiefly as an artist. It is said that revolutionary philosophers and political pamphleteers have most influence when they are giving expression to thoughts which are already stirring in the minds of their readers ; Delius's favourite selections from Nietzsche flattered and confirmed opinions which that self-willed young man had formed for himself, commended the life of artistic independence and, fortunately for us, were written in a language whose beauty, however vague its symbolism, intoxicated Delius and inspired his most ambitious musical conception — " A Mass of Life ".

Fenby, who detested Nietzsche's influence on Delius, writes :

Already as a youth, when he had left Bradford on his first visit to Florida, Delius was at heart a pagan. A young mind that had been nurtured chiefly on detective stories and penny dreadfuls was not likely to forget that incident he had witnessed in Bradford when Bradlaugh had stood, watch in hand, calling on his Creator to strike him dead within two minutes if He existed ! One wet day a few years later, Delius was looking for something to read in the library of a Norwegian friend with whom he was staying during a walking tour,

---

[1] Some materials from the present writer's article, " Nietzsche, Wagner and Delius ", in *Music and Letters*, vol. xxii, No. 3, are incorporated in this chapter.

and had taken down a book by one Friedrich Nietzsche ; he was ripe
for it. That book, he told me, never left his hands until he had
devoured it from cover to cover — the poison entered his soul.

Delius would have thought and behaved much as he did,
with the same love of travel and adventure, the same contempt
for physical or mental weakness, the same intolerance of other
people's religious or artistic opinions, the same haughtiness towards social inferiors, the same delight in wine and food, had
he never opened the poison bottle ; even that stoic endurance
of extreme affliction which would have impressed Nietzsche as it
did the Christian Fenby, as we are impressed with " Joy, shipmate, joy, pleased to my soul at death I cry ", did not come from
any reading or speculation, but from the fact that the composer's
character, though it may not have satisfied Cardinal Newman's
concept of The Gentleman, reflected traditional chivalric traits
begotten of pride, fastidiousness and the money to supply the
right taboos in childhood. They were part of the education of
several generations of Deliuses. He had the aristocratic virtue
of physical courage to a tremendous degree ; and we have
mentioned several aristocratic traits which, if not vices, are at
least generally thought selfish and unsocial. Wagner the man,
who endured not the slightest discomfort without reactions
which a whole household, if necessary a whole continent, had
to feel, was as much a disappointment to Nietzsche as was Wagner
the artist. He was vulgar ; Delius would have been Nietzsche's
idol had they been friends, but Nietzsche's philosophy commended itself to Delius just because it was the projection of
Nietzsche's temperament, and Nietzsche happened to be an artist ;
his supermen were artists, and he envisaged a fine new culture
which exalted the artist as its leader. The artist was never
allowed to pity himself. Delius was no intellectual ; he was
incapable of following any speculative thought that did not
flatter his own inclinations and rebellions, and the artist always
has been a rebel, even if a wise and accommodating Pope has

been able to harness his pagan delight in creation to the services of the religion of humility. Only a fool would suppose the favourite books from Delius's elegant shelves to have been more intellectual than the thumbed volumes of poor Schubert, whose taste in verse has been the jibe of several snobs.

Delius went Nietzschean for reasons which drive one youngster to Marxism, another to the New Yoga and another to the Buchmanites — it happened to be in the air, as a reaction to former hypocrisy or injustice. " The future lies in the hands of the sons of Prussian Officers ", wrote Nietzsche just after the Franco-Prussian War. (Note the social basis of the new culture ; the " haves ", the supposedly " strong " of nature.) Those young people were in the audiences with which Delius mixed ; they heard his first music ; with them, he experienced Wagner. " They were all speculative aesthetes . . . let us be pagan, let us taste life, escape, freedom, light ! " After the wool business, the kind of art admired in Bradford, the kind of Christianity professed in Germany or England during Delius's boyhood, Nietzsche's cock-shying was music to the rising generation ; but to a sensitive man like Delius, the language used was music in a permanent and therefore valuable sense of the word.[1]

If we are to understand the symbolic language used in Delius's master-work, " A Mass of Life ", which is taken from Nietzsche's *Thus spake Zarathustra*, we are forced to acquaint ourselves with a few of the leading doctrines of that teacher. Nietzsche fortified himself, and thereby the sensitive and artistic soul who opened his books and became a disciple, with nothing but the same final comfort that religious teachers have always offered as a last bone to those who are too shrewd to believe in

[1] An interesting parallel to the impact of Nietzsche on young Delius was confessed by the critic and philosopher Herbert Read in his broadcast talk on the Third Programme February 9th 1947. Mr. Read was very strictly brought up, first at a Yorkshire farmhouse, then at an orphanage. He had been " out in the business world some three or four years " when, at the age of nineteen, he first came upon *Zarathustra*. No single book, he says, ever caused him such a mental crisis : but whereas Nietzsche led Mr. Read to other philosophies and writings, he was an all-sufficient Messiah for Delius.

other nostrums — courage ! Placed in a world not created only for artists, and therefore a hard and lonely world at times, artists may meet pain of body and perplexity of mind. They have the sense to fall back on courage for themselves, but are soothed, even inspired afresh, when it is served in Nietzsche's magnificent prose, or, for that matter in the finer parts of the Hebrew bible or the Christian gospels. We do not know whether to blame Delius or his upbringing that he missed the Song of Solomon or the Book of Job, where he would have found that older religions had their bacchanal, and that " the morning stars sang together and all the sons of God shouted for joy ". He would have found it said of Messiah that " the dew of thy birth is of the womb of the morning ", just as he would have found between the same covers that even Solomon in all his glory was not arrayed like the lilies of the field, and that the words came from a Jew so fiercely patriotic, so physically strong, so like a Nietzschean super-man that, angered because a set of swindlers were disgracing his race by cheating visitors to his national capital, he whipped them from their place of currency exchange.

There are those who still talk of Nietzsche as the arch-rascal, but the musician wonders what all the pother is about. If that kindly scholar could see the cruelties and stupid revivals of ancient heresy which a little learning has attributed to him, he would be shocked. Much in his writing seems noble ; to artists, the best seems to have a great deal in common with the poetry of other religions. Nietzsche cried what so many poets of courage have cried, though they have not been put on the poisons cata-logue. Consider only the poets whom Delius used for musical settings, and who are respectable contributors to school an-thologies. Henley, who wrote some drivel about being the captain of one's soul, was pumped into us under the rod of a churchwarden headmaster ; and what is the substance of Shelley and Whitman, whose lines are quoted from pulpits ? Look at a sample text from *Zarathustra*, and we may be reading something from Confucius, the Bible or Mrs. Eddy. " Open thy heart to beauty." (" Consider the lilies of the field ") " Lift up your feet and forget not to dance for joy ; all laughter I pronounce holy." In the Apocryphal Acts of St. John, Jesus says : " Dance with me. Ye who dance not, know not what we know ", which holy bacchanal Holst used in the " Hymn of Jesus " when Delius preferred to get it from a rebel. " My head hath its coronal, my heart is at your festival ; dance round me, let me hear thy shouts, thou happy shepherd boy ", sings Wordsworth, perpetrator of the Ecclesiastical Sonnets.

Delius missed the joy of the older mystics and visionaries ; what he might have caught from Blake, Wordsworth or even St. John of the Cross, he happened to catch from Nietzsche — fortunately for us, for we are enabled thereby to have Delius the visionary as well as Delius the dreamer. Nietzsche himself was both. He denied that he offered the means of escape ; he insisted that he offered courage, but he deceived himself. His nostrums were (1) escape by adventure, by travel, physical and mental ; (2) escape by belief in Will and artistic Destiny, whatever that means ; (3) escape by pagan hedonism. In other words, there is little difference between the " courage " which Nietzsche offers, with extra fortification from a bottle, and the courage offered by Calvin without the bottle, except that the Deliuses have a chance to follow the Nietzschean way while the poor Mozarts and Schuberts have not. Like every preacher who tells us the last one was a humbug, and that escape is a superstitious delusion, Nietzsche offered what priests of every religion have offered, and he sang particularly beautiful music, and envisaged particularly attractive ceremonial to hide the mixture as before. Heaven was snuffed out for the prospect of " one great final destiny ", death by Zarathustra's midnight (tolling bell and all), sacramental wine for the intoxication of Dionysus.

Artists fired with religion often attempt to express the doctrine as well as the poetry, and suppose that what inspired them will inspire others ; that is why " A Mass of Life ", which keeps to the poetry and symbolism, succeeds throughout its length, whereas the shorter " Requiem " obtrudes the stuff of controversy and didacticism, supplied in words by Frederick Delius who, being a musician and not a poet, could not dress it in the haunting cadences of Frederick Nietzsche. But we should no more object to the texts because we are anti-Nietzschean than we should object to " Gerontius " because we dislike *pompes funèbres* and have shares in the local crematorium. Musicians have no more need to know the doctrinal teachings embraced by Delius than they have to acquaint themselves with the philosophisings behind Wagner's music dramas. They meant something when Shaw first wrote about Wagner ; nowadays only the music remains.

There have been Nietzsches since the world began, some calling themselves Hindus or Catholics, or orthodox in some way, some detected and pitched out as heretics. Many practising or professing Christians who would furiously deny discipleship of Nietzsche, talk and act in a Nietzschean manner — " I keep myself to myself ; I am the captain of my soul," etc. The difference between what Nietzsche teaches and what older religions taught may be seen by considering a man standing in a bucket, the bucket representing the life of man upon earth — " nasty, brutish and short ". The Christian says he cannot stand in the bucket and lift himself up ; he therefore believes in and appeals to a power outside the bucket. Nietzsche, as tired of the talk of the man in the bucket as he is of any power outside it, denies the external power and condemns as weakness the prayers and appeals. He advises one to enjoy the sinful bucket. His practice, especially as a medical orderly during the Franco-Prussian war, may have been at variance with his theory, for he was no hedonist or bully, but an amiable, self-denying scholar. Despite his counsel to enjoy the bucket, the poet gazes in rapture at the skies and the unattainable above the bucket — the same skies which receive the rapturous gaze of Christian, Buddhist, or corybantic voodoo. " *O quanta qualia sunt illa Sabbata . . . illic ex sabbato succedet sabbatum, perpes laetitia*", sings Peter Abelard. " Joy craves for all things endless day, eternal, everlasting day ! " sings Nietzsche in the words which close Delius's Mass ; and who, on musical grounds, cares a fig for the doctrinal differences ?

The bacchanal joy of Zarathustra often sounds sadder, more " escapist ", than the joy of Christian mystics, and so does Delius's music ; what with Abelard was nostalgic joy for the heaven of which we are not in entire forgetfulness, becomes in Delius the bitter-sweet enjoyment of a beauty which must fade before its rapture can be fully drunk. Of this element in art Nietzsche himself was aware ; it may explain what he felt, and then did not feel in the music of Wagner. This he called the " Dionysian " spirit, and it is profitable to see what Nietzsche meant by the term. His musical criticism is worthless, but his Hellenic studies were brilliant, and he has been admired by modern Hellenists both for his revelation of the religious, Dionysian origin of tragedy, and *pari passu* his championing of the virility of the sixth century in Greece, neglected by the older, Weimar classicists who, like Winckelmann, were familiar only with the art and drama of the fifth and following centuries.

In his lectures at Basle University, Nietzsche contended that, for all the perfection of Sophocles, the tragedy of Periclean Athens lost the " Dionysian spirit " of the age of Aeschylus and Pindar. In *Ecce homo*, he professed discipleship of Dionysus, god of wine, fertility and music, and in an appendix to that book wrote the poems called " Dionysos dithyramben ". The orgies of Dionysus, with his attendant satyrs and leopards, are described in the *Bacchae*, known of course to former scholars. It was Nietzsche's brilliant contribution to scholarship to trace in the Dionysian orgies the birth of tragedy ; there is not space to discuss here his account of the evolution of the tragic hero, but we may quote :

Either through the influence of narcotic drink, about which primitive men speak in songs, or the powerful onset of spring . . . awake those Dionysiac stirrings in whose climax all that is subjective vanishes in self forgetfulness — the bond between men and men is joined again. Change Beethoven's Song of Joy into a picture . . . when the millions sink into the dust you shall approach Dionysiasm in which, singing and dancing, man expresses himself as a member of a higher community.

In this ecstasy, man says " yes " to all life as it is. (We common people feel like that only when drunk, but to be a Nietzschean one must either recapture these feelings when sober, when faced with the task of orchestrating with twenty staves, or else fall back on — courage.) The deluded Christian does not " yea-say " all things ; he separates good from evil.

This yea-saying ecstasy is " *Die fröhliche Wissenschaft* ", the Joyful Wisdom or the Joyful Nonsense as you please. Zarathustra is Dionysus in the new culture, of which Wagner ought to have been the prophet, for only a musician could fill the role. Tragedy declined because Euripides and others moved away from the spirit in which it was born, and introduced the unmusical, un-Dionysian elements brought into Greek thinking by the spoiler Socrates, the " theoretical man ", who condemned music and put forward systems of argument and ethics. This inartistic culture was that of Athens, made supreme by the Persian wars ; she did not nurture the art of barbaric Greece whose " horizon was encircled by myths ", whose life was in warfare, tyrants, tragedy, music and orgies of Dionysus.

Sculpture, not music, was the main art of Periclean Athens, apart from talking and arguing. Sculpture is the art of Apollo, as music is the art of Dionysus. The Greeks, having lost their virility and begun their ethics, could not find life bearable without external support, such as the Christian postulates. They turned to Apolline art, which is similar in effect to a dream, " for Apollo is the god of dreams. They created a mythical artistic world, the beautiful Olympian world of gods and heroes. They set their minds on the art of outward appearances, with its fallacious but pleasing suggestion of a world order of similar beauty, meaning and symmetry " (A. J. H. Knight, *Nietzsche*).

Now for us to decide what in music is Apolline and what is Dionysian, although we may all agree that music is the most Dionysian of the arts, is as stupid as for Nietzsche to decide that *Meistersinger* was virile, and that the mutual welcomings and quarrellings of the Valhallan heroes were not. Since Nietzsche turned to *Carmen* after disappointment in Wagner we need not bother about his musical tastes, though they were sincere. He reacted against Wagner not merely because that refreshing rogue had discoursed during a walk upon the consolations of the Protestant Communion Service, but because his art did not come up to promise. No doubt Delius's art would have been the very music of the new culture, but even in the Mass we find predominantly Apolline as well as predominantly Dionysian moods. Let us have done with those sonorities and say that on some pages we have Delius the visionary, whom we shall meet in " A Song of the High Hills " and in " Songs of Farewell ", side by side with Delius the dreamer, endeared to Englishmen by " The Walk to the Paradise Garden ", " In a Summer Garden " or the humming intermezzo in the middle of " Brigg Fair " ; among our nature mystics we have room both for Wordsworth the visionary and Keats the mystic ; we can love both in Delius.

Delius's most grandiose conception, " A Mass of Life ", not only shows his highest visionary and artistic powers, but also reveals the limits of his musical and mental range. We cannot but find absurd Heseltine's suggestion that it is " a mass to stand beside the great Mass of Sebastian Bach ", but we can agree that it should be heard more often, and that it suggests performance " as a solemn ritual in some gigantic open air theatre, year after year at the coming in of summer ". We are taken spiritually farther by the first Kyrie of Bach's B minor or Mozart's C minor Mass than by the whole of Delius's, Elgar's, or for that matter

Wagner's, output. It is unfortunate that no clearer words can
be found than " spiritually farther ", but they are based not
only upon the testimony of people who have religious reasons
for liking to hear a mass. If lofty intentions, the desire to take
us a huge distance spiritually, were the criteria of greatness,
then Liszt and Mahler would be greater artists than Bach and
Beethoven, and one could mention a list of works at random —
single songs such as Brahms's " Oh Death how Bitter ", or
Warlock's " The Curlew ", or the best of Wolf, single chamber
works like one of the last Beethoven quartets, or Bloch's quartets,
single pages from the " St. Matthew Passion " — which take us
into regions beyond any invaded by Wagner or Delius, though
it will be noted that only one work mentioned is that of an
orthodox Christian. The others are by pantheists. One judges
a musician by his music, and in doing so, one declares that the
Mass is Delius's longest work, not his greatest.

It contains no markedly inferior music from the Delian well ;
on the other hand it contains much of the best. But we do wrong
in supposing that, because of its size and conception, it stands
head and shoulders above the rest of Delius's music as the " St.
Matthew Passion " or the Mass in B minor stand apart from other
works we know by Bach, or as " Messiah " does from other
Handelian oratorios. In the works just mentioned, the themes
treated brought that access of inspiration which made the composers surpass themselves technically and expressively. Delius's
Mass is more powerful in places than anything else he wrote, but
not more profound ; it impresses us by its length, its choral and
orchestral magnificence ; the " Songs of Farewell " have as much
to say, and say it with less adipose tissue, lovely though that
tissue is, while " Sea Drift " is more perfect in its poignancy, its
perfection of utterance and its judgment of effect.

The Mass is laid out for chorus up to eight parts where
required, four solo singers and orchestra. There is little contrapuntal or antithetical choral writing ; the voices are needed

(*a*) because they are human, and this work is the apotheosis of human life, not divine condescension ; (*b*) because they can declaim or meditate upon the words ; (*c*) because they can be added or subtracted for the sake of effects, just as masses or blendings of tone ; (*d*) because they make available an extra range of " orchestral " colour. Hence they are " doubled " as are orchestral instruments, and the composer is more interested in different types of texture, choral, orchestral or mixed, than in the varieties of linear weaving in one type of texture, the traditional contrapuntal choralism. (A more detailed study of Delius's treatment of the chorus will be found in the chapter on choral and orchestral works.)

The opening item is one huge choral dithyramb apostrophising the Will, as guide, captain and desire :

Ex.1   Orch.

Thou will un - bend - ing,   Dis - peller

thou   of   care

Thou   will *etc.*

Not the least merit of this chorus, which bursts in without introduction, is that, as will be noticed, there is the strength of crossrhythm (Example 3) and recalcitrant discord, especially in the bass. Consequently when this succeeds to the lush harmonic writing which is most characteristic of Delius, he can build it to a climax all the more moving, as Elgar does, by reserving his characteristic " Nobilmente " writing (Example 2).

A short baritone recitative bids all men lift up their hearts and share the joy of nature in laughter. " This crown of the Laughing One I set on my head. . . . Be like the wind when he darts from the mountain tops, who will dance but to his own whistled tune." The rhythm breaks into 6/4 time and the chorus joins in what becomes a dance movement. This second

section, one of nine which follow the opening chorus, shows one
phase of human mood, one age of man, one aspect of human
activity in relationship to his fellow men, to women, to nature,
to Zarathustra, his Dionysian self. The choruses are therefore
the counterparts of the tableaux in medieval plays like *Every-
man*, which depict the movement of human life from the cradle
to its " Destiny ".

Thus, in section three, we meet man as lover, and Delius very
finely offsets his voluptuous muse :

with the greatly relieving diatony of the dance-chorus :

DELIUS AT THE AGE OF 40

The last extract shows how, in this double chorus, Delius even turned to his purpose the contrapuntal methods of academic choralism. But it is absurd to call the piece " a magnificent double fugue ", and to pretend that the composer could have written elsewhere in such a form had he wished to. The effects are not those of a fugue, and where cumulative, the chorus is not fugally cumulative. Delius does not require that sort of defence, which is as silly as the Mozartian criticism that tries to present Mozart as a man with Beethovenian ideals but born too soon for them to have been acceptable.

For dialogue and for commentary soprano, alto and tenor soloists are needed, the voice of Zarathustra being depicted by a baritone. In the next two sections we see Man after his first youth in the struggles and joys of artistic growth ; the chorus work is therefore vigorous, rather than luscious and " typically Delian " like the gorgeous movement which follows. First " 'Tis gone, the lingering sorrow of my spring-tide. Summer I am become on mountains' high summits. Like a sudden tempest comes my bliss and brings me freedom " ; the solo voices bring their trio to a climax at " This is now our home — on the heights ", and the chorus ends on the cry " Wax ye hard ! " Then comes the rapture of Man's noon-day of com-munion with all nature, all men, and Zarathustra : " Glowing noontide sleeps on the meadows. O solitude of purpling heather ! O infinite bliss ! Lo, the golden rounded ball ; is not this moment perfect ? Who art thou, my soul ? " With this rich, somnolent chorus, the first part of the Mass ends.

In the second half the music must deal with the inevitable autumn and the knowledge that all must pass. Since Delius's music is at its loveliest in an autumnal atmosphere, we need not worry at the verbiage required by the Nietzschean text to slide past the facts of old age, pain and death. " Whither is time fled, have I not descended into deep wells ? The hound bays and the moon shines. Rather will I die than tell you what my heart at

F

midnight ponders. Spider that spinn'st around me, cravest thou blood? The dew is falling and the hour approaching which asks insistently: Who hath the heart to face it? What, livest thou still Zarathustra? O my companions, the evening filleth my soul with doubts, forgive my sadness." The midnight bell tolls, and we are to suppose that Zarathustra can exult solemnly because midnight " is the hour of initiation, when the soul may take wings and soar into the higher regions which are its home ". Yet of this Delius makes the most glorious music of all. Zarathustra declares " I am a drunken lyre, the lyre of Midnight. Thou art gone O time of youth, O noontide ! Then cometh Midnight ", and the chorus, to a beautiful sombre lilt, murmurs of Midnight : " Ah how she sighs, how she laughs in her sleep, how she moans, this drunken poetess. Her grief she swallows down in dreams, and if her grief be deep, yet deeper is her joy." The baritone begins the final section : " Come, now let us wander. Let us walk into the night. Ye higher-born mortals, the midnight hour is nigh." The chorus joins Zarathustra : " O man, mark well what tolls the solemn midnight bell ! The world is deep and deeper far than day can tell." Only by musical processes and growth could we find ourselves moving, with no apparent disjointedness, from this to a huge paean of joy : " Deep is her woe, but joy is deeper than grief of heart. Joy craves eternity, unending everlasting day ", on which ecstasy the music recedes, seeming not to end at all ; as Heseltine puts it, " in the last echoes all the voices of creation seem to utter the word Eternity ".

It is difficult to believe that this closing section was completed as long ago as 1898 and that it was included in the 1899 concert at St. James's Hall as a separate work with the title " Zarathustra's Midnight Song ". Perhaps the rather naïve echo of the words " midnight bell ", seen in Example 6, is one of the details which would not have come from Delius after he had written the rest, yet it must be declared that this final movement

is one of the most satisfying of all, and one of the most impressive of all Delius's choral finales.

If one takes a score of the Mass to one's room, not only does
the text seem to be a mere string of images with little core of
meaning, but the music seems to be a procession of chords with

Ex. 6

varying signatures, punctuated by moments of rest on chords
marked *ppp* and played with tremolo bowing. As we try the
pages over at the piano, we discover only the effects gained by
the usual means in the usual choral and orchestral score. The Mass
intoxicates and overwhelms even people with whom Delius is
not a favourite ; the audience is surely caught up, as Nietzsche
and the composer would put it, in the Dionysian inspiration of
the work, or as most Englishmen would put it, by its breadth
and vision.

It is customary in these islands to be generous with the word
" mystic ", to confer it upon anyone who has a vision and can
express it, and hence to regard all great musical artists as mystics.
We use it as Nietzsche would use his word " Dionysian ". To

be a mystic — to communicate what cannot be described but only experienced — one must use imagery ; that is the language of symbolism, by which bursting buds are symbols of the spiritual resurrection, falling leaves of human decline and death ; snowy peaks of human aspiration and rapture. The images of music are more subtle ; true, they are sometimes single chords, phrases, rhythms ; but the symbolism of music cannot be separated into elements like harmony, rhythm, tonality, melody. Critics have shown, by tracing the development of one finger-print, one idiom, throughout the work of a composer, that his response to a certain spiritual experience often calls forth the same musical symbol, and that more than one composer will seek the same sort of symbol. With Delius these musical symbols were sometimes used to the point of obsession, and then they can be roundly condemned during a study of the score at home. If they prove reach-me-downs when we hear a work as intended by the composer, mannerisms may be condemned altogether ; if we are deeply moved, though a given idiom has been heard a hundred times before, we have no right to carp.

It is not mannerisms which make Delius's " Requiem " an unsuccessful work. Failure of the language is the root of the musical failures between its covers. Just as it would be easy to parody the " musical symbolism " of Delius, as many have parodied the idiom of Franck, it would be easy enough to make nonsense of the language that inspired him. Most readers and listeners are moved by mystics who use one set of symbols but fail to gain any vision from another. We may thrill at Palestrina and find Beethoven's Mass either elephantine or tongue-tied ; we may react to Fauré and dislike Mahler, to the Book of Psalms and not to Nietzsche. If we dislike Nietzsche's imagery we ask just what is meant by Zarathustra's joy wanting to join grief and crave eternity ; but we should not reject this as a vague nothing unless at the same time we reject Vaughan's " I saw eternity the other night, like a great ring. . . ." We should not be debarred from enjoying those passages of sweet sadness which pervade certain parts of the Mass, just because we think nonsensical the claim that this sadness is different from other brands as " knowing no pessimism ", whatever that may mean. The Mass is a tremendous work because in its imagery Delius found just what inspired his own particular type of musical imagery ; Nietzsche's prose is melodious almost to a fault ; Delius's music is sweet to a degree which most continental critics think faulty ; Nietzsche makes one image come fast on the heels of the last ; Delius strung his rich chords in a way overwhelming to us young musicians when we first heard them, since but one such chord, used as a modulation, not just for its own sake, sufficed one of the older composers for several bars of music.

The occasion upon which, and apparently for which, Delius's " Requiem " was performed, and its unsuitability for that occasion, have already been discussed in the biographical part of this study. Nietzsche's language is missing, and the text no more resembles that of the Mass than does a pulpit exegesis the fine passage of psalm or prophecy it seeks to elucidate. We are spared the difficulty of explaining the symbolism, as we are in the Mass, but we are also spared a good deal of that music which gives sufficient experience to a musical soul to make him forget to read programme notes which purport to explain. The language of the " Requiem " might be the programme notes of the Mass.

One cannot agree that this work is quite so bad as some writers tell us, those writers being keen Delians. One has not had the opportunity to hear it, but judged by home-study it seems to be a grand work spoilt. Had its score not been printed, Delius might have shortened it, rewritten it and made something fine of it. It has parts of surpassing beauty ; the opening, for instance, is noble in a way not often found in the music of Delius. Its theme is the inevitability of death and the weakness of delusions about death as the gate to new life. The solemn march, to less " juicy " harmony than usual with Delius, puts us in mind of

Brahms's " All flesh must perish like the grass ". The words make a similar parallel : " Our days here are but as one day, for they are rounded in a sleep and ne'er come back again ; we are as a day that is young at morning ", etc. So far so good. Then follows the hint of coming queasiness and didacticism. " Why then dissemble with a tale of falsehood ? The weaklings wax sore and afraid ; they have drugged themselves with golden visions" (as Nietzsche and Delius never did!) "and built themselves houses of lies to live in ; then came a mighty storm with winds which laid it low ", and the violent music is at variance with the opening march.

In the second section there follows a sermon against ortho-doxy and delusion, in which the composer says " You are dead " with as much common sense as one would show by saying to a sightless man " You are blind ". For this purpose Delius must needs have two choruses singing together — the one the " Halle-lujahs " of initiates going gaily to death, and the other " the voices of the mob ", shouting " La il Allah ". How could the original audience know what this was about ? Needless to say the music is both poor and uncharacteristic of the composer. The next section, for solo and orchestra, beginning " My beloved was like a flower " has passages of true Delian beauty, though one may question its aptitude in such a work. But the final section is both noble and fitting. Just as Binyon, in the poem chosen by Elgar for the same purpose, sings " At the going down of the sun and in the morning we will remember them ", Delius evokes the beauty of times of day and seasons of year, the sun and the spring, to be regarded with poignancy for the dead that know it no more. Elgar's heroes were " straight of limb, true of eye, steady and aglow ", and Delius sings :

Ex. 7

Baritone

I hon-our the man who can love life, yet without base fear can die

With an accompaniment of strings and glowing horn notes, the baritone solo declaims : " His soul has ascended to the mountain-top that is like a throne and towers above the great plains which roll away into the distance. The sun goes down and the evening spreads its blessing, and so creeps on the night that is death's twin brother". And the passing spirit sings : " Farewell, I loved you all ", and the voices of nature answer him, " Thou art our brother ". The chorus enters with the words " Everything on earth will return again in endless renewing ", having the poignancy of " They shall not grow old as we that are left grow old ". It has already been pointed out that Elgar's chosen poem is not specifically Christian, nor is the greater part of Brahms's " Requiem ", so that need be no reason for our turning from Delius's to the other works. With or without an implied Christian doctrine, music can deal more forcefully than any art with the mystery of death and separation, more so than " Lycidas ", " Thyrsis ", " Ave atque vale " or a dozen of our other fine elegiac poems. That, but for his doctrinal obsession, Delius could have treated the theme wonderfully is shown by his supreme " Sea Drift ", if not by the fine opening and closing sections of the " Requiem " itself.

CHAPTER NINE

THE ORCHESTRAL WORKS

IT is by his orchestral works alone that many people in this country know Delius, keen though they may be to hear the great works for chorus and orchestra. Orchestral pieces are not so costly to produce ; unfortunately they take less time and trouble to rehearse. One has even heard the remark that if the strings are allowed to be slightly " sticky ", as they are prone to become in this luscious music unless firmly held, the resultant dawdling and sentimentalising will suit the music ! Beecham's taut, live rhythms and clear tonal balances are the answer to such nonsense, since Delius once declared that only Beecham understood his music. Proceeding on the assumption that a study is best made from the better known to the less known, it has been thought wise, after giving place of honour to the " Mass of Life ", to make notes upon the orchestral pieces before studying what are undoubtedly greater achievements.

Moreover it will be convenient to speak of the orchestral works in psychological rather than chronological order, with the tone-poems first and the concertos last. No finer introduction to Delius's writing could be found, no better example of his most characteristic conception and method, than the fantasy " In a Summer Garden ", dedicated to his wife, Jelka Rosen. Within the covers of that score are sections which are not sectional, changes of tempo, texture and mood which cohere, and passing impressions which differ as the flowers, the seasons, the times of day. The contrasts are as great as between the composer's orchard, the sunny walls, the paths and the river ; they blend as the colours and vistas of the old garden at Grez ; they open, fade and pass as the glories of the year. There are moments of silence, as in the " Siegfried Idyll ", than which gem the Delius fantasy is no less superbly organised, with an inner growth like that of a plant rather than with the technical joinery of scholastic form. The music seems to linger upon each mood and leave it with reluctance, but is ill served by any conductor who cannot hold the passing music, preventing disintegration and sagging while allowing its wayward flow. The short rests need careful judgment.

The sighing phrase which begins the piece and recurs in melancholy resignation towards the finish is quoted in Chapter Twelve, Example 58. It expresses our sweet sadness in the presence of beauty and our reflection that it must fade as the flowers. No one glory of the garden may stay except in the memory, nor can the heart drink all its glories at once. A second quotation, made at Example 60, illustrates the quick change of the eye from one thing to another, for this music is made of scrappets suggestive of the movements of birds and insects, the shrill of crickets or swallows, the flash of butterflies. In it is the dance of spring, the glow of summer, the morning and evening mists of autumn ; but of all lengthy portions the most appealing is that which seems to apostrophise the river, Example 8. The original garden was in France, but every sight, sound and odour, implicit in this music that defies analysis, is part of our English inheritance. The lazy Loing is taken as some native Avon, Ouse or Medway. Should one say " Lo here " or " Lo there ", one's finger would traverse the whole score, bar by bar, pointing to felicities of instrumentation.

The scoring is in no part like French impressionist technique. The entire orchestral palette is used — three flutes, double wood wind, cor anglais, three bassoons, bass clarinet, full brass with tuba, drums, harp and glockenspiel — yet no passing ecstasy is coarsely expressed. One can no more easily imagine Delius

using the restricted orchestra and ultra-refined scoring of Debussy's " Après-midi " than one can imagine Debussy quoting

Ex. 8

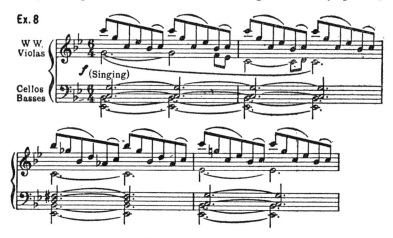

verse as blowsy as the Rossetti words which Delius inscribes on
his score after the dedication:

> All are my blooms, and all sweet blooms of love,
> To thee I gave while spring and summer sang.

" Brigg Fair " and " On Hearing the First Cuckoo in Spring "
are the pieces most frequently heard in England; no wonder
they are the favourites with the general public, for they, more
than their fellows, evoke the spirit of our English countryside.
Many musicians, including Beethoven and Dvorak, have left a
record of their feelings when afield. Delius has an effect upon
us different from theirs, in that there is always a horizon in his
canvas, or beyond it, so to speak; with Delius, we feel as we do
when reading Jefferies or Hardy, English writers who identify
our thoughts with those of a human pilgrim contemplating and
aspiring to such a horizon. In the choral settings of Nietzsche
and Whitman the horizon and quest are partly mystical and
spiritual. In these favourite orchestral poems they are unmistakably the beloved skyline of our English fields, woods, rivers,
hills, dawns and sunsets. That is why these works are popular;

the casual listener is at one in feeling with his countryside and countryman.

Some words by Cecil Gray, in his *Survey of Contemporary Music*, are particularly applicable to these " English " orchestral pieces, despite the magnificence of Delius's choral works.

Delius, like Keats before him, has often been unthinkingly reproached for the almost excessive sweetness and over-ripeness of his music. It is as well to bear in mind that this very sweetness and sensuousness is perhaps the most noteworthy characteristic of English art. The purist who would condemn it in the music of Delius is at the same time condemning a great part of Shakespeare — particularly the early works — Marlowe, Beaumont and Fletcher, Ford, Herrick, Campion, Dowland, Purcell even, and indeed most of the great musicians England has produced. It is the very quintessence of the English spirit in art.

Typically English, too, is the practice of falling in love with a tune so that the so-called variations are echoes, re-presentations, the new harmonisations of the unspoiled melody. This is directly opposite to the practice of Beethoven in the Diabelli or Brahms in the Handel set for piano, where an unremarkable theme is chosen, as Capability Brown said, for its " improvement ". The humble pumpkin shall become the coach and six. The English way, for all its wealth of harmonic and instrumental clothing, makes the composer write passages which may be called intermezzi; these are needed for contrast after so many appearances of the beloved tune. One of the interludes in " Brigg Fair " is a lengthy and beautiful one.

Delius did not call this work a set of variations, but " An English Rhapsody ". The folk-song, telling of true lovers' meeting at Brigg in north Lincolnshire, was sung at the village of Saxby-all-Saints in that district, by an old countryman named Joseph Taylor, in the presence of Percy Grainger. That composer almost immediately used the tune in his *passacaglia* " Green Bushes ", also written in the English way of affectionate repetition, with varying harmonies and instrumentation. He then

made a choral arrangement, and both treatments of the song took
the fancy of Delius, whom Grainger visited at Grez, and with
whom he formed a close friendship. Delius's " Brigg Fair " was
written in 1907, only a year after Grainger's setting. The tune
is in the dorian mode, but to Delius that fact suggested a treatment
exactly as he would have given to a diatonic tune.

In only one place is the scoring a little coarse, though a
staunch Delian may say that this short section gives a glimpse
of the more garish things seen under flares at the fair. The
passage comes just before the lovely closing pages, but one feels
that the scrappet used, taken from the opening (where it suggested the sounds of field and hedgerow into which the lover's
song breaks), is too slight a matter for blaring augmentation by
trombones and tuba. On the other hand, one cannot join those
who cavil at the naïvety of the slow variations, Example 9.

Ex. 9   *Slow with solemnity*

There is mystery in the distant song played by trumpets and
trombones in octaves, and enhanced by the effect of the solemn
bell-strokes and the off-beat chords on richly divided strings ;
we feel that the lovers stand together contemplating the night
landscape after they have walked away from the fair-ground,
and that their thoughts are set on life's mystery and on the
prospect of their own life together. Only a very censorious
person, meeting the phrase in Example 10, would deny Delius's
right to use brass alone, even in such a metre and at that brisk
pace, for the high spirits of a fair-day.

Ex.10 *Gaily*   [Full Orch.]   (Brass) *f*

The loveliest part of " Brigg Fair " is the interlude which corresponds with the tranquil " river " section of " In a Summer Garden "; it resembles that section in texture, and is marked to be played " slowly and very quietly ".

Foremost in the mind of musical English folk, when the name Delius is mentioned, is the work for small orchestra " On hearing the first Cuckoo in Spring ", which may be recalled with its companion-piece, " Summer Night on the River ". These little gems are the quintessence of Delius's utterance in pure contemplation of nature. Despite their shortness they are not mere impressions or miniatures. What does it matter that the chief melody in the " First Cuckoo " is derived from a Norwegian folk-song,[1] or that the ear must strain to hear the cuckoo notes in the middle of the piece ? The spirit is entirely English, and the cadential part of the tune, hauntingly and lovingly reiterated with never the same harmony, shows the English technical method. Phrase after phrase repeats with no more consciousness

Ex. 11

of technical formality than has the thrush that " sings each song twice over ".

Ex 12

[1] " I Ola dalom " (In Ola valley), harmonised by Grieg, Op. 66.

Careless poets and novelists have sometimes written as if, when alone with the beauty of spring, our mood is one of continuous ebullient happiness such as reflects the vernal landscape ; but our great nature mystics, and more modern poets like Edward Thomas, show that our mood more frequently turns to one of sweet melancholy.   Thus, though the first chord (Example 13) evokes the first warmth of spring on our spreading countryside, as no other composer could have done, neither the scene nor the cuckoo is the *raison d'être* of this music, but a human being — one of us, like the boy in " Sea Drift ", " absorbing, translating ".

By contrast, " Summer Night on the River " includes a large measure of direct depiction. Harmony and texture are exquisitely nebulous, so that we are aware of the river mist, " the unforgettable, unforgotten river smell ", the rocking of a small craft, even the midges and scarcely audible noises of the warm night.   Inevitably, even in a poem of such small dimensions, comes the flowing tune, set in the same quivering texture used for similar interludes in " Brigg Fair " and " In a Summer Garden ". The 'cello solo, despite its hazy setting and unhasting song, can hardly be said to share the luscious somnolence of its counterpart in the other pieces just mentioned. It was a stroke of genius to use the same method but so to conceive harmony and mood that the mysterious atmosphere of night should be retained.

For similarly small orchestras is " A Song before Sunrise ", a fine little pastoral which cannot quite claim the unique perfection of the two pieces of 1912, written six years before. The final section is a recapitulation which makes the whole a ternary form, but it needs imagination to accept the reprise after the brooding middle section. The change is artistically too sudden. It is as if the early rising wanderer afield ceased to sing his joy at the first light of morning, fell a-musing for a short time, and then dismissed his contemplations to resume his first song and stride. A delicious introductory section recalls those little noises and first stirrings of nature so well described in Stevenson's paragraph about the experience of sleeping afield. One feels that Heseltine was sufficiently impressed by " A Song before Sunrise " to emulate its form and spirit in his " Serenade to Delius on his sixtieth birthday ". The fact that no experienced listener, still less the connoisseur, would mistake Heseltine's sincerest form of flattery for Delius's own writing bears witness to the idiosyncrasy of the older composer's writing in all moods.

It is a pity that the " North Country Sketches " (1914) are not better known, for they are a little treasury of Delian orchestration, and in them we have in small space quite a compendium of his instrumental technique. As much could be learnt from this little score as one learns about Tchaikovsky from the score of " Casse noisette ". Little of this music can be conveyed to the mind through score-reading eyes unaided by memory of the sounds. In this respect, Delius's scores are more secretive than even Debussy's or Sibelius's, and it is no small wonder that the appearance of divided strings — for long passages Delius uses twelve lines of score for string parts alone — with harp and woodwind figurations, often reminds one of Debussyist technique but sounds quite unlike anything from that school. Delius often sounds best in passages which are not impressive on paper ; with Debussy and Sibelius what looks interesting usually sounds interesting.

The " North Country Sketches " have been elbowed out of programmes in favour of pieces which give us more of the all-pervading Delian voluptuousness, but these little works are rich and vivid in their own way, and it is deplorable that they are not favourites with orchestras of their country — Delius's own native north country. The popular Delius works have a tune which can be hummed ; that is why " Summer Night on the River " takes longer to become popular than its companion

piece. If a tune is necessary to popularity, only one of the
" North Country Sketches " will achieve it ; this is not one of
the three impressions of nature's moods, except indirectly. It
is the intermezzo called " Dance ", which gives a bright, if
legendary, atmosphere after the melancholy of " Autumn " and
the sharpness of " Winter Landscape ". Yet even the wind
sighing in the trees of " Autumn " has an implied song, and
throughout the sketches are hints and nuclei of tunes. The
most brilliant piece is the final " March of Spring ", which
exploits the full orchestral palette.

We now come to those orchestral works which, unless the
composer's intentions have eluded us in some places, are not
concerned with a background of wild nature. Perhaps for that
reason the quality and distinctive personality declines as we
trace this music in the order chosen. Of the two Dance Rhapsodies, for instance, it is hard to form a very high opinion. The
earlier one, 1908, is the more popular because of its bewitching
tune, and after the tranquil introduction it seems as if we are to
have another " Brigg Fair " ; some of the presentations of the
tune are rather like some of the treatments of the Lincolnshire
folk-song, but the whole is of much inferior quality. The jerks
from one variation to another, even with the help of transitional
pauses, cannot be manipulated by even the best conductors to
produce an effect of complete cohesion. And though there is a
second element in the tune, the work lacks the fine interludes
which connect the variations of " Brigg Fair ". The rhapsody
contains enchanting passages and seems to have roused enthusiasm
when Delian technique was a novelty ; but who nowadays
would endorse Heseltine's dictum that the penultimate presentation, given to solo violin above divided strings, is " perhaps the
most intense and exalted moment in all Delius's work " ? The
present writer never found it " wonderful, causing tears " ; in
fact the rhythmic alteration of the tune seems contrived, *faisandé*.

The second " Dance Rhapsody " is rarely played, but it is

DELIUS AT THE AGE OF 54

better welded. It does not, like its predecessor, consist in repeti-tions of the dance tune, for the main subject is in mazurka rhythm, articulated and treated sectionally. Probably because of the respite from lengths of triple tempo, or just because it is a later work, this piece holds together very satisfactorily. It was composed in 1916 and dedicated to Norman O'Neill, though it had to wait for its first performance until Sir Henry Wood's promenade season of 1923.

" Life's Dance ", the revision of a piece entitled " The Dance goes on ", has failed to hold public attention, though it was one of those works played in Germany and elsewhere on the Con-tinent when Delius's music was in the first stages of recognition. On the other hand, " Over the hills and far away ", called revolu-tionary and generally disliked when Haym played it in Elber-feld, is still in the repertory. It holds well together in spite of its early date and tame harmonies. It is usually called an over-ture nowadays, though when it was used to open the 1899 Delius Concert at St. James's Hall it still bore the title " Fantasia ".

An exception to the generalisation that works which do not look at open country are inferior to those which do is the noc-turne " Paris ; the song of a great city ". This piece has recently derived extra popularity from its selection for treatment as a ballet — miscalled, since the stage presentation is a matter of posturing and gesturing by a fellow about to finish his agony by jumping into the Seine in his nice cloak and hat. Though written a decade before the " English " tone-poems, " Paris " has something in common with them ; for though one con-templates the city at night, as from a roof-top or bridge parapet, or while wandering through deserted embankments, streets and squares, as did Goldsmith in his " City night piece ", one is made aware of what Hardy described as the spin of the earth under one's feet, just as is a night wanderer in the country beyond the city limits. Such contemplation and moodiness make a " nature " poem in some sense of the word.

If a trifle too long, " Paris " was the first fine orchestral work to come from Delius's pen. It is of ambitious range, and though Delius's brooding over the city has not the singing quality of later poems, it is remarkable that a work written when symphonic poems were the latest fashion should have little formal affinity with works listed in this category in musical treatises. It has no cyclic themes, no Straussian programmatic order. Its harmony and orchestral technique have just the slightest elements of likeness to romantic German music of the period. The German audiences, among whom Haym and Buths tried to get a first footing for Delius, expected a certain kind of music, and it says much for the appeal of his very different music in " Paris " that, though previous pieces from him were not wholly admired, these listeners, with their notoriously conservative and analytical outlook, were enthusiastic over " Paris ". That powerful appeal has commended the work in London, though it has not been taken to heart in the city of its title.

Together with a texture more German than is anything else from Delius, may be felt the first glow of his sensuous, " English " harmony. The scoring for bassoons, clarinets in the chalumeau register, and for dark instrumental tints in general, makes a sombre masterpiece, and there is something ominous in the heavy climaxes for full orchestra. The sincerest appreciation of this piece can be shown by declaring that it expresses all that is implied by the description " Nocturne ", and by its sub-title " The song of a great city ".

A similarly lengthy and diffuse work is " Eventyr ", with the sub-title " Once upon a time ", intended to evoke the atmosphere, scenes and characters from Scandinavian folk-lore in Asbjörnsen's tales. In these days when the public wants orchestra and still more orchestra, seeming to have no time for choralism or chamber music, it is surprising that " Eventyr " is not given as frequently as some of Strauss's tone-poems. It cannot be its dark and sinister passages that keep it out of the repertory or else we should not hear some of the popular Sibelius tone poems. " Eventyr " is just the piece with which to test a conductor and put the orchestra through its paces. It is a mine of effects and eldritchery, with shifts of mood, tempo and texture ; it is scored for a band of Straussian dimensions, including sarrusophone, bass flute, bass clarinet, drums needing two players, glockenspiel, celesta and a full " kitchen ". One supposes that, when scoring the meditative tone poems, Delius first conceived the string harmony and main effects, pencilling in any wood-wind lines he wished to stand out as solos, to recede or advance at certain points, or to give characteristic changes of colour. The wind writing in " Eventyr " is virtuosic, as full as the string texture ; the typically Delian string passages make constrasts as strongly as in certain Sibelius works, perhaps to depict parts of the folk-tales which are set in a sunny atmosphere. That " Eventyr " contains plenty of full-blooded Delian harmony, but is not typically Delian all through, is one of its many merits.

If " A Song of Summer " or the " Caprice and Elegy " for 'cello and orchestra were made out of that old material which Fenby was told to inspect when he first arrived at Grez, then the composer's musical powers were in no decline, for his sense of form is masterly. Little would one suspect that these pieces had to be dictated a few bars per day, a process which would rob any but a master of his grip of form. They are both ripely Delian works, though they have no distinct character of their own. In their mellowness we miss the occasional acid bite in harmony and scoring which offsets so many of Delius's richest pieces. Since a similar mellowness can be found in the last writings of other musicians, the smooth flow may be natural to one for whom the storms of life are over ; and as each passage was " played back " by Fenby the smoothing process may have been applied in a way which would not have been used on longer paragraphs. The pieces show those critics to be mistaken who, noting the natural diffuseness of Delius's materials, suppose him to have had no mental survey of a work as a whole. His grasp of form is extraordinarily sure in any inspired work.

Few of the concertos are at a level of inspiration for very long stretches. While recognising that Delius's essays in concerto do not attain the quality of his other instrumental works, it must be remembered that scarcely a single work in the form that achieves supreme merit fails to pay tribute to classical procedure. Concertos in rhapsodic style need not necessarily be inferior to those which respect the equal footing of soloist and orchestra, the ritornellic principles of older tradition ; but to write a concerto of any great length wherein most advances of movement depend upon the soloist is a task of extraordinary difficulty. Symphony and tone-poem reversed or disregarded the structural sequence of former classics ; not so the successful concertos.

Rhapsodies for solo instrument with orchestra may contain the rich mysticism of Bloch's " Schelomo " or the fine poetry of Vaughan Williams's " The Lark Ascending ", but concerto is weighted with heavier responsibilities ; to claim the title, a piece is not to be judged upon the sole merits of its emotional or spiritual power, nor upon its excellence as music. Structural magnificence must be an integral part of its appeal. Where is the concerto of supreme merit whose soloist is first cause and continual dictator ? No wonder that few composers since Mozart have written concertos to one-quarter the number of their symphonies. Most nineteenth-century concertos which hold their place are single examples of their composers' ventures in the form, written at infinite pains. Brahms, vindicating the classical procedures, is the notable exception. Elgar's 'cello concerto, more classical and less rhapsodic than his violin concerto, is the better. Concertos by the younger English composers very markedly restore the orchestra to a place of importance in the organisation.

Seeing that the principles of classical structure are utterly foreign to Delius's nature, we may admit that the finest music

in his concertos is the most purely rhapsodic ; therefore the
violin concerto is better than the others. Even in this work,
Delius cannot write one coherent rhapsodic flight of lyricism
from start to finish. Who could ? He is forced to find substi-
tutes for the variety and contrast of classical ritornello, though
he did not know the fact in such terms. Denied advancement
by metabolism, germination, or apotheosis of themes, he uses
sudden adventitious changes of time and texture. Only once, in
the 'cello sonata, did he write a sustained length of rhapsody in
which the soloist is sole dictator.

Were the violin concerto condensed, its best parts knitted
better, and the whole called " Rhapsody for Violin and Or-

chestra ", its glorious fare would be more tastefully and satis-
fyingly served. How arresting and beautiful is the opening,
Example 14, and how one could admire the way it plunges *in
medias res*, eschewing the paraphernalia of classical imitators, did
it not at the same time eschew the chance of germination by
cross reference and interplay, possible only when introductory
material is ritornellic. Within a mere eight bars he changes
tempo and gives us a second
theme in 12/8, knowing the
need for such duality. Then,
after the first big sweep of
bravura, and just before the
slow section (there are no

breaks between movements), he introduces short fanfare-like
themes for brass alone, Example 15, thus compensating for
ritornello. No less than ten times the phrase punctuates

the music, unaltered except in key. The interruptions are not ugly or inartistic ; they are essential and welcome, especially the innocent change to a dance in 12/8 which relieves the rhapsody before it returns for the final section. The pizzicato and extreme lightness are just what is wanted.

In short, any point in the work delights the ear ; the passages of accompanied cadenza are masterly ; the slow movement is of intense beauty, and Delius's own violin-playing taught him to know the instrument better than do most composers. If we listen as keen Delians, the violin concerto will not disappoint us ; if we seek a concerto, we shall carp.

The least successful and least Delian concerto is the double concerto for violin, 'cello and orchestra, written just previously to the violin concerto of 1916, and finished in the same year. It is hard to think of any motive for writing such a piece than the desire to answer a challenge. In all music there is but one fine example of this combination of instruments — Brahms's double concerto in A minor, triumphant result of a tremendous, almost superhuman effort of a type poles apart from that used by Delius in his greatest works. Counterpoint and cross rhythms of classical practice seem essential to such a concerto ; with Delius the 'cello impedes rather than enhances the violin, and it is strange that echo effects between the two solo instruments, or between one or other and the orchestra, which one would have thought particularly Delian, are avoided in a desperate struggle to get the 'cello heard from within its orchestral bed. There are laboured moments when Delius orders the 'cello to keep moving at all costs, and others when he seems to leave solo writing in sheer exhaustion and to give the orchestra the stage to itself. The orchestral passages are the best. Rhapsody, the chief source of beauty in Delius's works, seems denied at the outset of the double concerto by the very choice of instruments.

The 'cello concerto, 1921, being Delius's last essay in the genre, is more successful. It is written without breaks between

the movements. He knew the capabilities of stringed instruments, and although there is no evidence that he played the
'cello as well as the violin, this concerto contains fine writing
for solo display, especially on its opening pages. This is not
an absolutely first-rate work. The 'cello sonata moves in one
purposeful sweep ; the concerto soon lapses into the barcarolle
which is one of Delius's stylistic obsessions. The sheer sensuous
beauty of these lulling six-four passages beguiles us ; at a second
hearing we wish that the composer had a plan before scoring
such a lengthy work, for it is unthinkable that when he embarked
upon this middle section Delius knew even vaguely how long
it was to be. When we are taken out of it by something a little
more vigorous, Example 16, either the fresh breeze soon passes

Ex. 16

or some little figure is overworked, bearing no relation to previous
material. The extract shows the high tessitura for the solo,
though as a whole the concerto does not exploit it. Delius treats
the 'cello as he would a baritone soloist with orchestra ; the
other instruments play above it, of course, but they are always
accompanying it ; rarely do we hear it as a bass to the rest, or
as playing from within the harmonic mass. A fine and excep-
tional passage occurs, however, just before the end (Example 17).

Ex.17

As for the piano concerto, rarely has so wretched a plant
been rescued and nourished ; rarely has a great composer written

such drivel. We should not condemn it merely because there is
no good pianism to be found in its pages, nor because its composer was not a pianist. Even if the only keyboard tricks one
can play are such as require no advanced digital cultivation, one
has a perfect right to make any sounds from the piano that will
contribute to a piece which is worth hearing. This affair is
rabeted together. Let us not object to its leading tunes just
because one is ill-gotten out of *Parsifal* (Example 18) and the

Ex. 18

other from somewhere in the works of Grieg or Macdowell
(Example 19) but because they are the last things to sound good

Ex. 19

from a piano, and they are so shockingly botched together. The
lumping on of a final section to make a clumsy symmetrical
recapitulation seems to have been the composer's chief concern
in 1906, when he made into one piece the three-movement work
of 1897. Both in its pianism and its processional structure, this
work reminds us of those extracts from films, called by such
names as " Spitzbergen Concerto " or " Spumeshire Concerto "
or " Air-raid Symphony ", for which shrewd commercial
musicians have collected in short space the most obvious features
of romantic pianism. One has heard soldiers improvising showy
and sentimental fantasias for canteen comrades, and making as
good reach-me-down as Delius does write-me-down.

CHAPTER TEN

VOICES AND ORCHESTRA

THOUGH the name Delius is immediately associated in English minds with the " First Cuckoo " and " Brigg Fair ", it is essential to our survey of this composer's achievement as a whole that we recognise him first as a choral and vocal master. In doing so we must deplore the infrequent performances of the major choral works, and the poverty of the singing when they are attempted. Sir Thomas Beecham has received from musicographers the expression of our gratitude for his first twenty years' tireless championing of Delius, and for almost another twenty years' continuation of the good work since the Delius Festival. There is another man, however, who has never been much before the public eye, since he is not a regular orchestral conductor. Charles Kennedy Scott, lover of the sixteenth century, never let his flair for beauty be governed by a composer's repute. It is our luck that this great man and artist loved Delius's choral masterpieces ; that he is with us after another world war ; and that the Phoebus Singers show his ideals in an age of poor singing. Beecham himself was among the foremost to honour the name of Charles Kennedy Scott, having been impelled on several occasions, especially the 1929 Festival, to express his appreciation of the work done by Scott before handing over, for final rehearsal with orchestra, the finest choral body, both by selection and training, which has been heard in our time. Scott was, and is, exacting in his demands, and neither the singers of the Philhar-

monic Choir nor those of the Oriana Society would have tolerated
the storm of his anger — unusually severe even for a musician —
at what they thought adequate performance, had he not been
able to prove to them that they had previously no knowledge
of their own powers, and little knowledge of the composer's
intentions.

Unfortunately, Scott's standards and ability to reach towards
them are unique ; if he tried to form new choral bodies like the
Philharmonic or the Oriana, would this generation submit to
his whip ? Would it fill the hall for the performance of any of
the big choral classics ? Does that section of the public which
knew not Queens Hall in the twenties and early thirties recognise
not only that it has never heard a choral body of professional
standard comparable with that of orchestral teams, never heard
a crescendo more thrilling than that of the finest orchestra, a
pianissimo as intense and controlled as that of perfectly drilled
strings, but also that it has not heard even the English vowels ?
The few amateurs allowed by Scott into his choirs were such
only as regards payment or non-payment for rehearsals, and in
the smaller, more virtuosic body there were no amateurs in any
sense of the word.

Opportunity has been taken to pay belated tribute to Scott
chiefly because he made musicians see the folly of supposing
that Delius was unsympathetic in writing for choral forces.
Delius knew what he wanted and was sure of what he wrote ;
his most exacting demands are deliberate and truly vocal. Rarely
was this fact impressed upon us more deeply than during rehearsals of Delius's last great choral setting — Whitman's " Songs
of Farewell ". (Unfortunately neither Beecham nor Scott was
on the rostrum for the actual first performance. Despite in-
structions given by the composer through Fenby, who came
specially to England for the occasion, the conductor appointed
did not deign to learn either from Delius or Scott, and the slick,
commonplace performance could not compare with the revelation

of Delius's conception that had been evident at the choral rehearsals.)

Following the same method as has been adopted in other chapters, it would be profitable to study the " Songs of Farewell " first, though they are the most amazing of the dictated achievements of the composer's last years. In the first place, these settings use the choral forces throughout, without solo voices or any lengthy orchestral interludes ; in the second place, they are available for the student in a clear vocal score, and are as typical of Delius as any earlier work, in spirit, choice of words and treatment.

Though extensive quotation from so rich a texture would take abnormal space, even snippets can show (Examples 20 and 21) certain characteristics, one of which Delius has in common with Handel of all people. When that classical worthy wanted to bring off an effect by putting basses, tenors or any other voices in a certain register, he gave not a fig for rules of cadential approach, or for progressions within the parts as forbidden by theorists. So Delius, seeking a certain *sound* at a certain place, recks not whether, in eight-part writing plus orchestra, disapproved degrees of the scale are doubled, whether the bass is the true bass, whether the vocal texture could stand alone or whether one part must leap a proscribed interval. Nor, though the songs are for " double chorus " and orchestra, need we worry that the whole may fuse to only four, five, or six vocal parts, that parts may be doubled at the octave or unison, and that it never suits Delius's purpose, here or elsewhere, to write for genuine double choir, with Bachian or Handelian antithesis. It merely happens to be essential to Delian harmony that the parts of his choral force can be employed *divisi*.

Handel who, of all composers in these islands, knew what he was about when writing for voices, can also be used as a stalking horse as regards treatment of words. It is not the function of music, especially choral music, to nurse syllabic accent or

Ex. 20

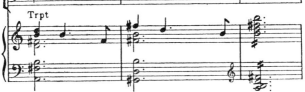

Ex. 21

quantity, and then to find a phrase that will put the missing jig
nicely into the rhythmic jig-saw. The concern of the musician
is music, of which the text is the inspiration and not the master.
Better Elgar's appealing music, even when the words are mis-
handled, than a D.Mus. exercise with donnish sensitiveness to
the words and merely respectable music. But the first-rank composer is rarely cavalier with his words. Let us recall the familiar
" For unto us a child is born ". To gain his main point — the
solid declamation of the Prophecy of the Four Names — Handel
has to set the opening words floridly, gradually bring in all four
vocal parts. Why does he select the last word, " born ", for
florid elaboration, rather than any other word, such as " child " ?
It is hard to say why ; but we cannot imagine the semiquaver
run elsewhere. So Delius begins No. 5 of the " Songs of Farewell " with careful regard to accent (Example 22), and in the
next line but one proceeds to the treatment seen in Example 23.
A glance at the vocal score will show that the latter procedure is
no less satisfactory than the former.

Finally one must repudiate those who think that Delius
asked for the impossible from singers. He never did, not even in
the " Song of the High Hills ". A high soprano C on the words
and in the places selected by Delius need be neither weak, ugly
nor out of tune. It is also risky to charge with writing
unvocal parts a composer who seemed to think in terms
of song even when writing for instruments. Delius often ob-
tained splendid effects by making voices do the accompanying
(Example 24) to offset those passages of entirely different conception, such as Example 25.

Either a composer gets the effect he intends or he does not.
If he does, we cannot call him incompetent, but we may dislike
his intentions, as we may quite justly dislike Delius's intentions,
though hardly in the " Songs of Farewell ". Concerning the
proud spirit of these Whitman settings there is little to say,
except that they are the last choral legacy of the composer who

Ex. 22

Ex. 23

wrote the " Mass of Life ", and that, when the arrival of his amanuensis made possible an Indian summer after the main musical harvest, nobody could have dared hope for grain so rich and still so vital as the " Songs of Farewell ".

Having seen the chief characteristics of Delian choralism we should pass to his most typical form of composition, namely

Ex. 24

Ex. 25

that which uses chorus, solo voices and orchestra, each in its own right, and each in relation to the others. Most critics think " Sea Drift " to be the most perfect among Delius's major works, and the opinion seems to have been unchanged since its first performance in England under Sir Henry Wood at the 1908 Sheffield Festival. Essen has the honour of the first performance, having selected the work for its festival two years before

Yorkshire, which county had never before heard its son's music.

Several reasons could be given for the perfection of "Sea Drift", apart from the plain one that Delius rarely wrote at so consistent a level of inspiration. ("Perfection" is a word one cannot often apply to a lengthy Delius work as one surveys the whole.) First we should notice that Delius never bent a text to his musical purposes in so masterly a way; his decision sometimes to let the baritone solo, sometimes the chorus, advance the story, at other places to make the chorus echo the soloist or just give it an emotional or atmospheric background, is made with uncanny judgment of the right times or places for one type of approach; none of the devices is overworked. The pathos of human bereavement, symbolised in the seagull's bereavement, could well have been expressed by this particular composer by means of orchestra or choir, separately or together, but one cannot now think of so poignant a medium as the baritone voice crying above, within and around the chorus and orchestra.

To find out what Delius wanted from Whitman, we should notice the difference between his and Vaughan Williams's selection from the series of poems entitled "Sea Drift" in the poet's "Leaves of Grass". Vaughan Williams took three of these for his Sea Symphony — an exultant work which swells our pride in the "Song of all seas, all ships", our solemnity in contemplation of the ocean at night, our delight in the play of winds and waves. Delius's aim is not a sea symphony, nor, directly, the evocation of any mood of the sea which affects the onlooker. The positions of man and ocean are reversed. The composer is concerned with a boy's first contact with the drama of separation, his first awareness of the fact of death, as he watches and "translates" the mating, nesting and happy life of two sea birds, until one of them fails to return. True, we are aware that "the wrinkled sea beneath him crawls", that "the winds blow

DELIUS AT THE AGE OF 69

up Paumanok's shore ", that the sea " surges hoarsely " under
the full moon in calmer weather, and that the lone singer sits
" down almost amidst the slapping waves " ; the orchestral
opening to the work immediately brings us to " the surgy
murmurs of a lonely sea ", and we are left with the same lonely
sea when the last " No more, no more " recedes. The sea is always
there, but the work is not a seascape. Delius's primary concern
is to express the emotions embodied in such lines as :

> Soothe ! Soothe ! Soothe !
> Close on its wave soothes the wave behind,
> And again another behind embracing and lapping, every
>   one close,
> But my love soothes not me, not me.

> Low hangs the moon, it rose late,
> It is lagging — O I think it is heavy with love,
> O madly the sea pushes upon the land,
> With love, with love.

It is worth while to be guilty of heartless prying in order to see
exactly what and how Delius selected and arranged from his
poet, for we shall understand what *type* of writing made music
well within him, and with what certainty he avoided any writing
that is not apt for his own musical clothing. (A point to be discussed at length in dealing with the operas. Delius's common
sense in choosing exactly *his own* words should be studied by
several modern composers.)

(1) He deliberately tops and tails Whitman's " Sea Drift ". As
    a result (*a*) after a phrase or two about the cliff grass in
    spring he reaches his main business — the " two feathered
    guests from Alabama " and their happiness together ; (*b*) he
    leaves the text on the poignancy of loss — " We two to-
    gether no more, no more " — knowing quite well that his
    is not the muse to match Whitman's philosophising on the
    subject of Death. One has heard literary people wishing

H

that Delius had continued with the poem. Not only would this have marred the present unity by making a distinct part two, with an entirely different kind of music, but Delius would have made a poor essay in that *kind* of music, were it possible for any first-class musician to deal with the subject of Death in any but an oblique manner — stating or reflecting merely. Were it in the nature of music to marry into philosophy, Liszt and Mahler would have been at the nuptials.

(2) Whitman carefully prints in italic the meditations of the boy, " absorbing, translating " ; he leaves in normal type the main narrative. Who but Delius would not have thought that this lightened the task of selection and arrangement ? Why not give the italicised material to the soloist and let the chorus connect the story, or vice versa ? With Delius the baritone solo is an entity, but the chorus is there to amplify the same sentiments as the solo. Though the chorus does add to the scenic background in some places, make parentheses in others, either in overwhelming splendour, as in :

or with quiet commentary in :

its chief function is to share the meditations of the boy, singing the same words as the soloist either simultaneously, or
more slowly, or as an echo.

Perhaps the most beautiful part of the work is reached when,
without orchestra, the chorus begins " O rising stars " and the
soloist breaks through with " Shake out carols ! " The lines
should be quoted to show what a perfect choice this writing was
for Delius's music ; its recapitulation of imagery, its echoing
and rocking to and fro of single words and phrases, are almost a
musical technique :

Shake out carols !
Solitary here, the night's carols !
Carols of lonesome love ! death's carols !
Carols under that lagging, yellow, waning moon !
O under that moon where she droops almost down into the sea !
O reckless despairing carols.

This tireless apostrophising and recalling, hardly found in
English-writing poets except Whitman, shows the use for
deliberate effect of a method which has hitherto been a necessity

to musicians, whether they think they are rid of the older imitative " development " or not. Nothing but emotional recapitulation could have imbued Delius's ending with the mixture of remembrance, despair and resignation to the words " O past ! O happy life ! "

Linked with this masterpiece of 1903 are " Appalachia " and " Songs of Sunset ", for both express the emotions of separation. The first was written six years before, and the other four years after " Sea Drift ". Heseltine has pointed out that at the words " Waters of separation surpassing roses and melody ", in " Songs of Sunset ", occurs the cadence of the theme in " Appalachia ", in which " the great river stands as a symbol of the poignancy of parting ". It is the slave tune, " Oh honey, I am going down the river in the morning ", a tune by every critical standard jejune and banal, which we cannot help remembering, as if it were a thing of beauty, after we have just listened to Delius's " Appalachia ". This work is always described as fifteen variations for orchestra and chorus upon a negro melody, but if one tries to listen to it as fifteen variations one is likely to be disappointed and waste a good deal of time. It is better described as " a long twilight brooding " upon the negro country and upon the theme of love and separation, especially since the big choral section comes after the " variations " to make an epilogue, and the most ambitious orchestral writing is in the introduction, which is the counterpart of the choral epilogue.

The negro song, not a particularly good one except as heightened in Delius's setting, expresses the feelings of slaves who could be moved from one Mississippi plantation to another, miles away from wife or children. Except in the final section of choral writing, the voices do not use actual words, but they enter pianissimo and round off the presentations of the slave song " almost as though the spirits of the forces of Nature invoked by the music became suddenly articulate ", and one cannot too strongly condemn the practice of omitting the choral elements in " Appalachia " — not so much on account of the main choral epilogue, but because of the loss of these " doxologies ", as Heseltine has called them.

No musical quotations are made from " Appalachia " ; a sample specimen would look so simple, even immature, just as a line of the song looks like doggerel. Delius thought very highly of the work and it must have some peculiar quality about it, some attraction that cannot be explained musically. Though it is an example of mature writing (indeed it was a landmark when first composed), Delius's technique, harmonically, orchestrally and structurally, went a good deal farther than this ; yet it seems to be those very musicians who do not reckon Delius among their favourite composers — those whom one would suppose foremost in naming " Appalachia " a work of more promise than achievement — who regard it as a work for the performance of which they always wait with interest. When Heseltine went through his temporary reaction against Delius's music, when he grew out of his first intoxication and recognised the value of other, vastly different, ways of expression through music, there were hardly half a dozen works by the former idol in which he failed to point out defects or supposed defects. " Appalachia ", which any apprentice stone-thrower would find an easy target, he stoutly defended, as never failing to give him a deep spiritual experience. In view of these facts, it is not of importance that " Appalachia " interests the present writer only in one or two places, and that, however careful the performance, it always seems unable to bring off the intentions of the score. The chorus seems to make too sudden a change ; we are made aware of breathing, of difficulty in keeping intonation. Perhaps the score itself is not perfectly what the composer intended, though there is magic from the first horn calls and echoes along the river banks.

The " Songs of Sunset " constitute a lengthier work than the title suggests, for they use the same forces as the " Requiem " — soprano and baritone soloists and a very full orchestra. The

movements, from the opening " A song of the setting sun ",
move to climax of a type which superficial inspection would
hardly call climactic. Delius's peroration is vastly quiet, as when
" the evening is spread out against the sky " and night descends
on valley, woods and hill. A fuller, richer, choral and orchestral
harmony than has been used before surrounds both soloists for
the final poem : " They are not long, the days of wine and roses ;
out of a misty dream our path emerges for a while, then closes ".

It will be seen that " Songs of Sunset " deals with the same
theme as the " Requiem " — the beauty of life and its transience
— but without the didactic queasiness. Its unity of feeling is as
sure within the musical texture as in the cycle of poems ; and
our sense of its flow towards the final " sunset ", despite the
reversal of usual climactic methods, bears witness to an inner,
organic unity like that of " In a Summer Garden ". That Delius
was a certain judge of this is shown by his excluding from the
cycle Dowson's best poem, " Cynara ", whose words Delius
set to music for baritone and orchestra and published separately.
The " Songs of Sunset " therefore make one of Delius's finest
and also most characteristic works ; and when the present decline
of choralism has passed its worst stage we may hope to hear it
among the first Delius revivals. It could have been used instead
of the " Requiem " as Delius's tribute to the fallen in 1919 ;
Dowson's title to the first of the poems chosen for " Songs of
Sunset " was " Moritura ", and Delius's commentary on death
is amply implied in his music ; he made himself no more explicit,
only a little tiresome (as he was in conversation when he tilted
at religions other than his own), in the " Requiem ". The
one piece meditates and the other tries to speculate, thereby
divorcing the functions of music and words, and making one of
the two unnecessary. It is Delius's musical meditation and commentary that alone attracts musical and non-musical people to
him ; without that, he is not even competent as a musician ;
for all his superb competence is directed to fashion music to that

one spiritual purpose ; change the purpose, and there is no general ability which can turn out a Mass to-day, a ballet next week, and some piano albums next year. William McNaught speaks of Delius in general [1] with words that are particularly applicable to the " Songs of Sunset ".

His orchestral and harmonic imagination were one, and from their fusion sprang the very terms of his musical language. It was not a language that lent itself to the articulate phraseology and designs of symphonic music ; nor did it promote rhythmic invention as ordinarily understood ; and in the setting of words it tended to deny the activities of speech. . . . His music is a world in itself, limited when one regards all that is excluded from it, but limitless in its height and depth of visionary effect and suggestion.

The words summarise the whole argument between those who idolise and those who minimise Delius — his limits, spiritually and technically, and the limitless vision once he is on his own country. " Songs of Sunset " all lie in Delian country and in its richest province.

In no other score by Delius does choral writing reach a more " orchestral " conception than in " A Song of the High Hills ". The whole work has the shape of a peak ; it opens on the lower slopes in triple lyrical rhythm wherein Delius's ranging pantheism makes little parallel with Beethoven's " awakening of happy feelings on reaching the country ". Instead we have a series of emotional and spiritual experiences such as might accompany a day's mountaineering. The song-like opening changes to quiet tensity during the first vistas of ascent, becoming more and more animated until the heights are reached. A tremendous exultation, expressed by the orchestra in full splendour, passes, with echo effects among the instruments, to the quiet rapture of divided strings. At this spiritual climax the voices take over, at first seeming to come from the far distance, while the quivering strings soar to the thin heights of their speech, and bring the snow-capped summits before our eyes.

[1] *Modern Music and Musicians*, by W. McNaught (Novello).

The picture as such, that is to say as a sensory rather than a spiritual experience, recedes when the strings fade into mist and the voices take over, necessarily at a lower pitch and more solid tone, despite the mark *pppp*. The voices are concerned with human emotion rather than musical photography ; they cease as we leave the heights, and the orchestral music of descent is made of materials heard during the ascent.

Though harmonic and instrumental procedure may seem very similar in two Delius works for the same media, it is extraordinary how every great work by this composer has its unique character. " A Song before Sunrise " is quite unlike " On hearing the first Cuckoo " ; " Brigg Fair " is quite unlike " Paris " or " Appalachia " ; and though a sample of the wordless choral writing in " A Song of the High Hills ", for instance Example 28, seems to use exactly the same chromatic progressions as many another chorus (cf. Example 24), nobody hearing the passage would put it by mistake into " Songs of Farewell ". We have a similar phenomenon in the wordless

Ex. 28

Ex. 29

folk-like song, to be sung by soprano and tenor in octaves at the climax of this work. Why, we say as we look at something with no more spiritual content than would give a pleasant legendary flavour to one of Grieg's piano pieces, should this fragment of local colour, " unvocal " in its repeating notes, seem actually to make vaster the vastness of the hill-tops, when we hear it in the Delius work ?   (Example 29.)

It is unfortunate that " Arabesk ", for baritone solo, chorus and orchestra, has disappeared, perhaps temporarily, from English programmes. It stands in relation to the deeply emotional " Sea Drift " or " Song of the High Hills " as does " Eventyr " to other orchestral poems, since, as its title suggests, it is a work of fancy rather than of pathos. Its neglect, like that of " Eventyr ", is due to our admiration of its composer as a mystic and nature poet ; we look to him for poignancy and exaltation, and overlook certain abilities which we might recognise more often and more practically in a composer of the second or third rank. We rarely think of Delius as an orchestral virtuoso, or as an artist of caprice and whimsy. We revel in the full chorus, the warm orchestral bed of horns and divided strings, the sagging or climbing romantic chromatics, but pass over pieces in which the chromatics are more mysterious and recalcitrant, the rhythms more gnomic, the scoring more sharp.

We may wonder whether the opening words of " Arabesk " brought Debussy's " L'après-midi d'un faune " into Delius's mind, albeit unconsciously. Within the opening pages, he limits his large orchestra to Debussy's instrumentation exactly — flûte, clarinette en la, deux cors en fa, etc. — to accompany Jacobsen's words :   " Hast thou in shady forest wandered ? Know'st thou Pan ? "   At any moment we expect a libidinous harp glissando, but although *les deux harpes* are there, they bide their time ; Delius's Pan is more sinister but less animal than Debussy's. Odd places are highly reminiscent :

Ex. 30 Fl. Solo

Ex. 31

But these similarities occur only at the opening. The piece is very fully scored, the orchestra including glockenspiel, celesta, harp and a large percussion department, as well as the extra bass wood-wind instruments for which Delius wrote so well. The chorus never takes full harmonic panoply in its own right, as in the " nature " works ; its chords are often stark in their use of octave doubling. The voices are just extra means of colour and suggestion in accompanying the soloist.

Delius wrote three fine works for solo voices with orchestra. The very full orchestra of " Cynara ", even in the animated parts accompanying " Flung roses riotously with the throng ", and " I called for madder music and for stronger wine ", never swamps the baritone voice. Though first sketched in 1907, the piece was finally dedicated to the memory of Heseltine, whose character seems pointedly associated with Dowson's words.

The vocal line pays unusual accentual respect :

Ex. 32

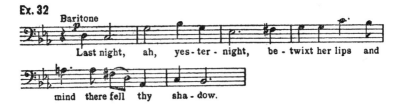

We cannot always tell the effect of Delian vocal line by singing it to ourselves. His treatment of words is not so cavalier as some people suppose ; he rarely violates their just accentuation in his mature work, and he is meticulous in the matching of musical to literary sentiment. The undulations of the vocal line must be judged in combination with what is going on in orchestra or other accompanying media. Consider, for instance, the following :

Ex. 33

If the vocal line had to stand alone, the double cadence would not be satisfactory ; at " in the air " we should need a different turn of the line from the drop at " happy life ". With Delius's harmony and orchestral flow at this spot, nobody wishes any alteration. Again, the words " But I am desolate and sick of an old passion. I have been faithful to thee, Cynara, in my fashion ", come as a poignant refrain after each strophe of more tempestuous music telling of the lover's mad vagaries ; naturally there are rhythmic echoes in the returns of this refrain, as on the word " Cynara ", but we shall note that Delius's musical refrain is not complete like Dowson's verbal one. Most other

composers would have repeated exactly, but we shall not find
that, by so doing, Delius would have achieved his effect any
more finely.

The chief unifying device in the already spiritually unified
" A Late Lark ", for tenor voice and orchestra, is the recurrence
of little wood-wind figures. The accompaniment is virtually for
small orchestra, since the trombones are used only as a soft bed
of sound, chiefly to mark the calm resignation of " So be my
passing ". This is a perfect little work, as is Henley's poem.

On a larger scale altogether is the " Idyll " for baritone,
soprano and orchestra to Whitman's words : " Once I passed
through a populous city ". In any but Delius's hands this music

would be as near in style to the clichés of musical comedy or
romantic film as are certain phrases in the Whitman verse. No

apprentice would dare use his themes so persistently without variation as Delius does (see asterisk in Example 34) ; no other composer would use materials so banal, or sentiment so direct ; but no other composer would catch us up so easily into the undying, unspent summer of romance. Otherwise how could we endure some of the stuff in the Whitman lines ? Consider the things one may do with love : (a) " I exhale love wherever I go ", (b) " I ascend, I float to the regions of your love, O man ! " But for the magic of Delius, how could we forbear to remember what the bishop said to the actress ?

Fenby tells us that some of the material for the " Idyll " came from the old one-act opera *Margot la Rouge*. There must have been parallel sentiments between parts of Mme. Rosenval's libretto and Whitman's words, which are those of a man reflecting on " A past incident ". Mr. Whitman, at the height of fame, had to go through a certain city ; it was the lady who made the certain suggestion. In an America yet innocent of mass nymphomania by correspondence, this creature is reported to have said : " I could not die till I had looked on you ". Though Mr. Whitman, like Mr. Wordsworth, had a very fine conceit of the importance and influence of W. W., the lady must have meant what she said, for she looked and then died, apparently satisfied ; we are not told whether Mr. Whitman had any temporary satisfaction from the irritations of public life, but we do know the heights of speculation and spiritual experience to which the poet was moved. The climactic words are " All is over and gone, but love is not over " — and whatever that means let him explain who knows ; for the present writer it means some incredibly lovely and rejuvenating music made out of some incredibly commonplace and hypocritical materials.

The populous city must have turned Delius to Paris, for he not only inspected *Margot la Rouge* but, in the lengthy orchestral introduction to the " Idyll ", wrote music strikingly similar to that in the tone-poem " Paris : the song of a great city ", both in its dark instrumentation, the brooding pedal-point, and even the principal theme :

Ex. 35

Mention must be made of Delius's single unaccompanied choruses, of which " The splendour falls on castle walls ", using horn-fifths in dying echo effects, and the two male-voice choruses " On Craig Dhu " and " Wanderer's Song ", to words by Arthur Symons, are the only pieces with words. Neither in these nor, as one might suspect, in the unaccompanied choruses, like " Midsummer Song " or the two little gems " To be sung of a summer night upon the water ", does one feel that portions of greater works have been cut out to make smaller. Each little work is a distinct personality.

This justifies our regarding Delius as a choral master, and there is no sense in saying that he *could* not write for voices as does Parry in his " Songs of Farewell ", or for strings as Elgar does in his " Introduction and Allegro ". He had no desire to do so. If his writing is unvocal, we need not quote so extreme a case as Wagner ; let us use the classical Brahms as a stalking horse. But for the different harmonic and structural idiom, there is much choral writing in Brahms, for instance in the " Song of Destiny ", the Alto Rhapsody, even the " Marienlieder ", which is not unlike choral writing in Delius. What we are entitled to complain of in the Delius choral works is not the nature of the choral technique, for if we dislike the technique, whatever the type of work, we might as well reject the work and the composer with it ; a cause of genuine complaint, how-ever, is the ubiquity of mannerisms, which show more in choral writing than elsewhere. On Delius's stylistic obsessions more is said elsewhere in this study ; particular instances in his choral writing can be traced even in the small passages used for music-type illustrations in this chapter.

CHAPTER ELEVEN

THE OPERAS

O F Delius's operas, *Irmelin, The Magic Fountain, Koanga, A Village Romeo and Juliet, Margot la Rouge, Fennimore and Gerda,* only two, *Koanga* and *A Village Romeo,* have been markedly successful, though the last two on the chronological list have been published. It will be seen, after an inquiry into the kind of story to bring the best music from Delius, that, printed or not, the last two operas — *Margot la Rouge* and *Fennimore and Gerda* — are much less likely to survive than the first two, which are still in manuscript. Both *Irmelin* and *The Magic Fountain,* though we know little about them except the general plot of their libretti, are stories with a semi-legendary and romantic setting, which would give them much in common with the two successful operas in the middle of the six, and bring from Delius music of the same vein. We have at least some support for this supposition. When Fenby arrived at Grez, much early work was taken from the shelves to see what could be completed or revised. The composer planned a good deal of re-writing ; the only part of the early operas to be rescued was the very beautiful Intermezzo from *Irmelin,* and since this has appeared in a piano transcription many readers will have marked its similarity in nature to the famous " Walk to the Paradise Garden " in *A Village Romeo.* Perhaps *Irmelin* may yet find production ; we do not know whether Delius withheld it from production himself, or whether its production was ever refused. In the case of *The Magic Fountain,* the composer demanded its withdrawal in 1893 after it had already been accepted by the Weimar authorities — an almost unparalleled act of self-criticism. A second pointer to the vein of both operas is the fact that Grieg liked what he knew of them.

Before examining the operas available for inspection, it is not just desirable, but necessary, to consider the difficult art of libretto hunting, together with the justice or injustice of the word " undramatic " as applied to various types of libretto and treatment. Throughout the history of opera, people have thrown either this word, or period synonyms like " artificial ", " exotic " and " irrational ", at the persistent efforts of writers and musicians to make works which have their musical art-form though they share elements with other arts. The point to be emphasised is that opera should not be judged upon its success or failure as a hybrid, *e.g.* whether its story is " good theatre " or not, but in its own right. The *procedure* of the music, the course of emotional appeal, derives largely from the libretto, but the musician decides where his work will move at the speed of ordinary dramatic action, or where that action will be arrested to make musical commentary or to draw lyricism from a situation. In simple terms, opera happens to need our eyes as well as our ears — our mind's eye, even in a broadcast performance. In judging the staging of opera, all we need decide as musicians is that the appeal to one sense is not at variance with the appeal to another ; any further concern with the stage is not a musical matter. Having relegated criticism of operatic presentation in its non-musical aspects to dramatic and literary critics (who cannot be the final arbiters of a musical form) we are concerned with the artistic coherence of the composer's work. He primarily is responsible for opera, and once he has begun shaping a libretto to his ends we are finished with the librettist unless he happen to be the composer. This applies even when a domineering librettist influences the composer ; whether the composer accepts or rejects advice, he is still to be praised or blamed for the result.

DELIUS IN 1927
His wife arranged a regular series of readers

Opera is as much a musical form as symphony or concerto ; that is why operatic failures are precisely those essays in which composers have been unable to find the right libretto for their own personal muse. *Prince Igor*, as disconnected and as unlike the work of a great playwright as is a Pageant of Empire in the grounds of Bangfrippet Castle, is also a magnificent opera ; but had Borodin obtruded his personality into operatic music by Mussorgsky, the result would have been even more objectionable than was Korsakof's transformation of *Boris*. Success does not depend by any means entirely upon the composer's intelligence or musical stature. In colourful, fanciful subjects, Korsakof was as lucky in finding the right stuff for himself as was Puccini in his melodrama or Mozart in " dramma giocoso ". Mozart might deceive the dramatic critic into supposing him the one composer able to move at the speed of Beaumarchais. The musician asks how on earth, if this were true — if Mozart merely gave Beaumarchais a musical clothing — could *Figaro* be published as a series of arias, duets, terzets, etc., with a dance and a march ? Why should the most poignant moments be those in which action is at a standstill and the Countess reflects, in a formal aria, upon a situation which was amusing when presented as a matter of comic intrigue but overwhelmingly pathetic once the human heart, banished from satire, comes into play ? At such moments we must judge Mozartian opera as we would Handelian or Wagnerian opera — by its effect ; if, in regard to any operatic essay, the average audience wants to use the word " artificial " (whether able to define the word or not), then either the audience is out of sympathy with the composer or else, as is most likely, it senses discrepancies on the composer's part to achieve his musical ideals, or to make them musically coherent.

There was no such trouble with the audience, either in the theatre or listening at home, when *A Village Romeo* and *Koanga* were offered to them. It is the theorists, not average audiences, who need to make effort to judge a work by the composer's

aims. The audience can enjoy *Igor* one day and *Boris* the next ;
unless given an unprecedented kind of entertainment, as at the
first performance of *Pelléas et Mélisande*, they are tolerant even
towards absurd and outmoded conventions. They go for the
music ; they are disappointed when the composer has not found
the right outlet for his own musical appeal.

Musical biography of the romantic epoch and of our own
experimental age shows composer after composer beginning an
opera, scrapping it or, if more conceited, having it rejected ; we
read of others who made plans and sketches, and persistently
read likely libretti. Granted that several works should be known
and are not, *e.g.* Wolf's *Corregidor*, the path is strewn with
finished and laboured works in which, unable to find the right
story, this or that composer belied his musical nature as did
Delius in *Margot la Rouge*, hardly a bar of which is truly Delian.
The second rank of composers — Humperdinck, Charpentier,
Puccini or Korsakof — with shallower muses needing only the
fanciful or the melodramatic story, were more frequently lucky
than the giants. Verdi, ultimately a giant, was the luckiest of
all, happy at the *Traviata* level because his musical growth had
reached that level and found its book, happy at the *Aïda* level,
and triumphantly happy at the summit of *Otello* and *Falstaff*.

This necessary digression leads to Wagner, since what best
suited Wagner's nature was the kind of tale that suited Delius.
This does not mean that there is nothing of Wagner in the early
operas with the ingredients used by Meyerbeer and Spontini, but
that Wagner's wrestling with the task of finding what he wanted
may have actually shown Delius a way and spared him a good
deal of trouble. Unable to find the right libretto, Wagner wrote
his own : Delius also did so for *Irmelin* and *The Magic Fountain*,
and made his own revision and selection when he used other
men's words. Despite the very different flavour of the music,
A Village Romeo is the same kind of opera as *Tristan and Isolde*.
Unlike Delius, who cared nothing for critics, Wagner was a

German who felt the need to cogitate and theorise — especially about the meaning of " dramatic ". How much does the music student, as distinct from the Wagner student, gain from that composer's lucubrations ? The music dramas themselves are the guide to Wagner's intentions, and very different is the practice from the theory. " *Ticht, Ton und Tanz* " indeed! Nature chose to make Wagner a musician, so love was crown'd and music won the cause — notably in *Tristan*, where little but *Ton* matters, however desirable it be that Isolde be reasonably slim and agile. Provided the bench supports the lovers and the ship tosses discreetly, we can enjoy *Tristan* with our backs to the stage,[1] for, as surely as the Fifth Symphony, it is a triumph of *musical* form, whether or not a literary man calls it undramatic. So much is music the first cause of *Tristan* that it has been said that if as much happened on the stage as in the orchestra, the work would be banned. It brought out the greatest in Wagner, and had Delius chosen to write a *Tristan* — a different and English *Tristan* — the story would have brought out the greatest in Delius.

What, in simple terms, is the kind of libretto for composers like Wagner and Delius ? First a legendary one, since such a story is already charged with romantic atmosphere, and these are romantic composers ; the mystery of distance makes the legendary figures into symbols and prototypes of all heroes, all lovers, who express the struggles and yearnings of all generations. Secondly, a tale which provides scope for the voluptuous and ecstatic, and contains between its lines more than the lines themselves can communicate without musical expression. Thirdly, a story in which some scenes present either the distances and horizons of seascape and landscape, or the romantic appeal of nature unclipped and unbridled, of storm, crag, ruin, forest or

---

[1] As the present writer did on first hearing the work. Having stood several hours outside Covent Garden to secure the cheapest accommodation, even youth objected to further standing. An occasional peep at the stage picture, to make sure that the music was passing through the proper hands, served to stretch the legs.

fen. Distance in time, or of horizon, draws music which is vast and general in its appeal, unfettered by the need to outline small objects and petty domestic conversations. The music of *Tristan* or of *A Village Romeo* is therefore in extreme contrast to Strauss's programmatic music.

We shall see how, even in song, Delius was attracted to Scandinavian poets just because nordic verse abounds with romantic legend, and Delius's best songs, such as " Irmelin ", " Twilight Fancies " or " Hy Brasil ", are set to the stuff of legend. No wonder, therefore, that *Koanga* and *A Village Romeo* are the best of the operas.

Let the best be first examined. The story of *A Village Romeo* is even briefer than *Tristan*, and comes from one of the tales in Gottfried Keller's *People of Seldwyla*.[1] As in Shakespeare's play, two families live in mutual hatred, but the friendship of the boy from one and the girl from the other ripens to ardent love. Contention between their fathers, two Swiss farmers, lies in their rival claim to a strip of wild land between their fields. They ruin themselves in litigation, and the lovers, Sali and Vrenchen, are penniless. The real heir to the disputed land is a vagabond who cares nothing for the claims. His name is deliberately withheld, for he becomes more symbolic and sinister by the appellation " The Dark Fiddler ". Determined to have one evening of rapture, the lovers go to a local fair, but the jeers of neighbours cause them to walk to the Paradise Garden, a dilapidated riverside inn with its beer garden neglected, overgrown — romantic. (It should be mentioned in passing that the piece we now know as " The Walk to the Paradise Garden " was composed five years after the opera, though using thematic material from the play as does the " Siegfried Idyll ".) A barge laden with hay is moored to the bank. The Dark Fiddler has arrived at the inn, which is hung with lanterns while he and a crew of disreputable companions settle there for a drinking

---

[1] A good English translation is published by Dent.

party. He invites the lovers to join them and follow the vagabond life. They decline the invitation. They plan to live out the evening of their happiness and, at its close, to die in each other's arms. Let the dialogue and stage directions finish the tale, for its ending is climactic in poignancy and beauty :

> *The rising moon floods the distant valley with a soft and mellow light . . . something mysterious has touched the garden with enchantment.*)

BOATMAN (*in the distance, gradually drawing near*) :

> Halleo, halleo ! in the woods the wind is sighing.
> Halleo, halleo ! downstream our bark is gliding.
> Heigh-ho ! wind, sing low, sing low.

VRENCHEN : Hark ! this is the Garden of Paradise. Listen, the angels are singing.

SALI : No, it is only the boatmen on the river.

BOATMAN (*nearer*) :

> Homesteads round about us scattered
> Where folk live until they die.
> Our home is ever changing —
> Travellers we a-passing by.
> Ho, travellers a-passing by.

S. : Travellers we a-passing by ? Shall we also drift down the river ?

V. : And drift away for ever ? I've had that thought this many a day. We can never be united, and without you I cannot live. Oh let me then die with you !

S. To be happy one short moment and then to die — were that not eternal joy ?

S. and V. :

> See the moonbeams kiss the meadows,
> And the woods and all the flowers,
> And the river softly singing
> Glides along and seems to beckon.
> Listen ! far-off sounds of music
> Waken trembling echoes, moving,
> Throbbing, swelling, faintly dying.
> Where the echoes dare to wander,
> Shall we two not dare to go ?
> See, our marriage bed awaits us.

They go towards the hay-laden boat. The DARK FIDDLER *appears upon the verandah of the inn, playing wildly on his fiddle.*)

V. : See, my garland goes before us. (*She plucks the nosegay from her bosom and casts it on the river.* SALI *jumps into the boat and casts loose.*)

S. : And I throw our lives away ! (*He withdraws the plug from the bottom of the boat and throws it into the river ; then sinks down upon the hay in* VRENCHEN'S *arms.*)

Boatman (*in the far distance*) : Ho, travellers we a-passing by !

The orchestra alone then concludes the work with a perfection unattainable by words ; the music can suggest the deep and enfolding waters. However much the pathetic emotions have been stirred, we are satisfied and comforted almost as by the " happy ending " of comedy. Such a beautiful ending is possible in opera ; music without words can suggest and express ; words without music in such a place can hardly do more than describe, and in the precision and realism of description lies the danger of crudity and bathos. The music can fade to rest ; words merely come to an end.

Opera-goers who require the stage properties and dramatic interruptions of Italian opera, the pageantry and ballet of Russian opera, the discrimination of character and emotional versatility of Mozartian opera, cannot fail to be disappointed in *A Village Romeo and Juliet*. No opera is more musical, because in no opera has the composer been more certain that by music he would tell the tale ; Cecil Gray has called it " a symphonic poem with the implicit programme made explicit upon the stage ". What words could be sung to the well-known sequences of Example 36 ? What changes of scene, lighting or colour could be made to advance and recede as do the various woodwind tone-colours in those phrases ?

In this work the opera-goer must expect only music, and music chiefly of the same kind — sustained, dreamy beauty, slightly offset by the sinister strains of the Dark Fiddler or the litigious quarrels of the farmers. That is why *A Village Romeo*

and Juliet proved so effective for broadcasting, by which medium
it is likely to become most widely known and loved.

Before making any observations on less successful operas,

we may note how, despite the experience of *Tristan,* opera pro-
ducers as well as the opera-going public were not prepared for
such conceptions as *A Village Romeo and Juliet* when they first
came to deal with it. Debussy made his position and theory
quite clear for the notorious launching of *Pelléas et Mélisande.*
People who hissed, disliked the theory as much as the practice,
but they had no opportunity to intrude elements of staging
which did not belong to the piece, whereas even Beecham made
the mistake of allowing a steam merry-go-round to aid " realism "
in Delius's opera ; the result was to obtrude something unreal,
taking us out of the real terrain of the music.

The trouble with other Delius operas is that Delius himself
took his own muse outside its proper terrain — or at least outside the country in which it shows its greatness. Of course it
was impossible for him to find a libretto in which romantic love,
pantheistic mysticism, and brooding upon the transience of
beauty, could be spun to three hours, and we must not suppose
it a defect of his work that he declined to give musical expression
to any parts of a story which did not suit his purpose. We
should be content to accept the programme note : " The same

garden, three months later. Jones has died of drink. Mrs. Jones thinks she drove him to it and has refused to see Smith, her former clandestine lover." We have no right to carp because most of *A Village Romeo and Juliet* consists of "Boy meets girl again", or because seven of the nine pictures in *Fennimore and Gerda* are unmixed love-scenes ; but we have every right to carp when Delius fails in a chosen task. For instance, in *A Village Romeo*, he seeks to draw extra lyricism of his own kind by depicting the dream of their forthcoming wedding which comes to Sali and Vrenchen as they doze at the fireside. They imagine themselves in the Swiss village church ; the bells ring and the organ plays, very glutinously and nastily, and the hymn sung by the villagers is one of the most sentimental pieces of pious balderdash, grand Amen and all, that ever took its revenge upon a man who had sneers handy for church composers. Perhaps Delius remembered the fine way in which Wagner used the chorales in *Meistersinger*, and we cannot doubt that his intentions were serious ; otherwise we should be forced to suppose that in this church scene he wished to parody religious music of the late nineteenth century.

Similarly, in *Fennimore and Gerda*, Delius himself was responsible for material which took him out of his best musical terrain. This was his last opera, and it contains stuff which, *pace* many critics, is even more advanced and well-written than the average page of *A Village Romeo*. We have not the same sustained enchantment and loveliness, for the plain reason that the story is in modern dress ; the composer denies himself the legendary setting, and Jacobsen's dialogue is substantially retained. The work is short and uses only those "two episodes from the life of Niels Lyhne" which are apt for musical treatment. It is divided into "pictures" which are connected by orchestral interludes throughout ; this does not make too long a sitting, for the whole opera finishes in one and a half hours.

The poet Niels Lyhne falls in love and cannot help declaring his passion to Fennimore, who is engaged to Erik Refstrup, a painter. Erik and Niels have been close friends from childhood, and when Erik and Fennimore marry, Niels clears off. All members of the triangle belong to the well-to-do classes, and this enables the scenes, or rather scene, with varying seasons and times of day, to be laid in their beautiful garden by a fiord. The marriage proves unsuccessful. Erik makes no headway with his painting ; the lazy and wealthy rarely do ; he spends more and more time with a set called " the Boon Companions ", whose chief boons are *le sport* and the bottle. Fennimore is neglected and writes to Niels, thinking that he may interest and influence his old friend. Niels arrives and there is much of the silly talk one finds in films which include " artists " (the whole novel should be a " find " for a film producer), yet the scene brings forth some of Delius's best music. Erik says he cannot get any inspiration, that his time at the easel seems wasted. Niels recommends travel, which may bring new impressions and new inspiration. But the influence of the Boon Companions is strong ; a demirep schoolmaster taunts Erik about his " immortal paintings " and persuades him to come with the rest to a fair at Aalborg. Niels promises the weeping Fennimore that he will stand by her. He does ; and the old passion flames up. While Fennimore is expecting him from his house on the other side of the fiord, a telegram arrives to say that Erik has been killed in a road accident at Aalborg. She rushes out to meet the arriving Niels and in her frenzy rails at him and herself. So far we have heard nothing of the other lady mentioned in the title, and for no reasons, musical or dramatic, can one explain the " Gerda " episode. Apparently Delius wanted a happy ending, though Jacobsen made Niels die in a military hospital. However, Delius decided to tack on to his opera a picture which shows us Niels on his farm in harvest time, in love with this Gerda, a girl still in her teens.

Naturally the best music in *Fennimore and Gerda* is that

which either enhances the scenery — the winter forests, the sea and fiord, the harvest, the summer sunset, etc. — or else bespeaks the surging of love passion, not the pantheistic rapturous passion of *A Village Romeo*, but the more direct emotion of " verismo " opera. That similar situations called forth the same musical response may be seen from the snippets quoted at Examples 37 and 38, the first a motif used during the love scenes, the second

Ex.37

Ex.38

accompanying Niels's words to Erik : " Reality to me is imagination ; one day I shall write really good poetry ". The difficulty comes when Delius feels called upon to keep music going during moments which would have been honey to Puccini. " Fennimore tears open the telegram, reads it, and totters backward. (*Sings*) ' Erik dead ! . . . thrown out of the cart. . . . His head is shattered.' . . ." Delius might have served himself better by the tactful method adopted by the sergeant sent to tell a wife that her husband had been killed in action. " Is the widow Refstrup in ? I'm afraid you'll find she is, madam." A production of *Fennimore and Gerda* cannot avoid Delius's own slips, but it is proof against the kind of producer who could cause bathos in the more rarefied moments of *A Village Romeo*, or the gentleman who, year after year, gave us that huge overhanging tree and ornamental cascade in *Tristan* at Covent Garden.

An enormous disadvantage of *Fennimore and Gerda* is the difficulty of translation into English. Heseltine does well, but he

is often too literal ; a typical instance may be given : Example 40
is suggested as being preferable to Example 39, though it takes
liberties both with language and music.

Koanga is a most interesting work to the student who wants
to examine the earlier work wherein Delius distilled the essences
which best served his later purposes.   At this stage (1895–97)
young Delius wanted a lively libretto, with plenty of colour
and pictures, a chorus, opportunity for dancing, whimsy, and
exotic atmosphere, as well as the rich sentiment of which he was
already finding himself the master.   *Koanga* is a hotch-potch,
but a lively one ; it would please the general public or the radio
listener as much as does drama of the *Chu Chin Chow* kind, and
it is a pity it is not broadcast again.

The Spanish slave-masters look forward to the arrival of
Koanga, an African chieftain, who has been captured by the
agents and should be useful on the plantation.   His spirit is un-
breakable, but they feel that the beautiful octoroon Palmyra
may act the part of a Delilah, and that her woman's arts may
bring him to accept the one bondage with the other.   But deep
calls to deep and Palmyra is in love with him, refusing the
advances of Don Pedro and Don José.   Her mistress is dis-

traught, and confesses that " she was my father's daughter ". Koanga takes to the jungle with other slaves, invokes Voodoo and Black Magic, and brings fire and ruin upon the plantations, perishing himself. Palmyra kills herself.

That the germs of real Delian music exist in *Koanga* most musical folk know from the popular excerpt, now recorded, from the wedding preparations for Koanga and Palmyra, at which the slaves dance the Calinda ; one of the chief themes shows an early version of that which is so movingly used in " The Walk to the Paradise Garden ", Example 41.

Ex. 41

Keary's words are sometimes fatuous and always crude, and though much has been said elsewhere about Delius's treatment of words (see especially notes on his songs and choral works) we may note that the vocal line is no more angular than is Wagner's or Debussy's, and that what looks angular when score-reading comes perfectly smoothly at a performance.   Like young Elgar, Delius had literary enthusiasm rather than literary taste, and the accentuation of 4/4 Ko- | AN - ga is our | HE - ro prince ; no | FOE we fear when | HE is nigh, is neither more nor less vulgar than Elgar's 4/4 | WE are the mu - sic | MA - - kers.   It is doubtful if in any other score from a great musician, anything so amusingly fatuous occurs as the work-song of the slaves in *Koanga*, Example 42 (B). Since Delius went to a school for the well-to-do, he can hardly have learnt such choralism from sources where, in our youth, we encouraged ourselves in song to " Dig out the weeds, and turn up the sod, And *spread* the manure as our teachers have shown ".

What one cannot hope to find in Koanga is great progress in that chief problem of composition which Wagner called " the art of transition ".   There is a vast difference between the

modulation to the key of the slave chorus in Example 42 (A) and
the modulations in *Fennimore and Gerda* ; neither modulations

nor other methods of transition seem to give much point to
passing words or scenes. In *Koanga* Delius just revelled in the
colour or emotion of contrasted pictures, in the tom-toms of the
Voodoo spells, the laughing choruses of the wedding preparations, the plantation songs and the love-making : to get from

one scene or mood to another was a tiresome necessity; the easiest method would suffice provided it was not too obviously at odds with what came on either side.

Margot la Rouge, lithographed but not published, was a one-act opera written for a prize competition with no choice in the matter of libretto, which was provided by one Mme. Rosenval. A soldier returns from campaigning to find his betrothed selling her favours in the cafés; high words, knife work and corpses are the rest of the story. Little time need be spent over a piece for which the composer had little time. It provided enough pages of the right kind of music for Delius to rescue material to use in the " Idyll " — " Once I passed through a populous city " — for baritone, soprano and orchestra.

Delius is said to have given much thought to the possibility of making libretti out of *Deirdre of the Sorrows* and *Wuthering Heights*. The first should have suited his purpose, though the Brontë story was the one which fascinated him most. He intended to make it into a series of " pictures ", as he had *Niels Lyhne*. It is most unlikely that his opera would have recaptured the spirit of *Wuthering Heights*, but we might have had a wilder and weirder *Village Romeo and Juliet*. At least both these tales are now semi-legendary; they have the romantic distance of time, place, and their own special world. It needed a Mozart at the supreme level and a Puccini at the melodramatic, sometimes meretricious, level, to make successful opera out of a subject not obviously romantic.

CHAPTER TWELVE

THE CHAMBER WORKS

To mention Delius's chamber works is to think chiefly of what he chose to call, and had every right to call, sonatas for stringed instrument with piano — hardly " and piano ". The surviving string quartet is an isolated phenomenon.

Pejorative criticism of the chamber works, for which one sees no justification, seems to be based upon the following statements, each of which has appeared at some time in the musical press :

(*a*) " These are not sonatas . . .", a remark so absurd that space should not be taken in its refutation. To the same mentality Sibelius's symphonies are not symphonies. As for the story that Delius knew not what sonata or fugue was or that he took no interest in technique, there is mention in the biographical section of one Thomas Ward, organist and Bach player, and of a young Delius, supposed to be orange planting, who spent his whole time in the study of technique. Throughout these and later days he was constantly at the piano finding the stuff of which music is made. Perpetrators of the story need reminding that Delius was an incurable leg-puller of so-called interviewers.

(*b*) " The piano part is no part at all " — neither is it in the songs ; and in Mr. Puff's words, " why the devil should it be, sir, in a free country ? " Let the main answer to this charge be implicit in that to the third.

(*c*) " Delius does not excel as a melodist." Retort to this is contained in other places of our study dealing with " The song

of a great city ", " A Song before Sunrise ", " A Song of
the High Hills ", " A Song of Summer ". Let any musical
person hear the opening of the first violin sonata, on the
records made by May Harrison and Arnold Bax, an opening
as lovely as that to any Brahms sonata, or as the enchanting
opening of the Franck sonata;   still more let him hear the
'cello sonata, which is one unbroken rise and fall of melody
(see Example 43), and then, considering how the piano con-

Ex:43 CELLO SONATA

tributes nothing melodically, let him acknowledge that the
ability to write a huge spate of melody alone made the work
possible.

The essential character of a Delius sonata [1] is that the solo
melody becomes the first cause and final arbiter, decreeing all
shades of dynamic intensity to an accompaniment which paces,
reflects and colours, but does not converse as with an equal.
There is little evidence of approach to this uniquely personal
conception among duo-sonatas of the nineteenth century. Even
Grieg wrote sonatas in which melody and accompaniment work
together to make some interplay ; the most to be found of interplay in a Delius sonata exists in a few echoes or ritornels, or a
few chords leading from one flight of solo rhapsody to another.

The homophonists who established the classical sonata
depended for architecture on related keys — at one time a
stereotype. Their melodies tended to be short adaptable frag-
ments waiting to be shuttlecocked between solo and accompaniment. In Mozart sonatas the melody keeps largely to the formal

[1] Material following is largely taken from the present writer's articles in the *Monthly
Musical Record*, January 1932, and the *Musical Times*, January–April 1935.

subjects (though with Mozart there are sometimes pleasant extras), and at least one of the subjects is a compound of figures such as will articulate for later treatment. The word "treatment" has no place in describing the work of a rhapsodic melodist like Delius. Only a fool would disparage Mozart's melody at its best or even second-best ; it shows unparalleled fertility in ringing changes on a metrical norm of the utmost simplicity. But it takes another fool to measure other composers' melodies by Mozart's. The term "homophony" implies that a melody is to be considered in its setting — something we should call static were it not that all good music flows, something enhanced by charmingly balanced surroundings in which it poses for admiration. Rhapsodic melody might, by comparison, be called kinetic. It rides over its setting in defiance of clutching harmonies when Delius is the composer. Mozart's contemporaries gave us what that age called "a prospect" of a boat on its charming or moody waters ; Delius demands that we go a-sailing.

What guide or critical standard has the rhapsodic composer ? For it was beauty of interval, rhythm, balance and sequential imitation that pinned homophonic melody for the ear to appreciate. Was it just the ear ? Surely a distinction of classical melody is that the mind's eye is brought into play, albeit unconsciously, and we *see* the tune in its frame. Rhapsody cannot be pinned, and of its nature even quotation must be lengthy ; it is hard to "get a specimen". Its enjoyment consists in sympathetic response to its movement *while it is moving*. Beethoven first transformed the older conception of melodic beauty to suit his dynamic purposes ; later came the prose-like rhythms of the *Meistersinger* songs, whose phrasing is decided by climax, not measures. Yet even Wagner's audience was able to retain the traditional habit of *seeing* structural arrangement beneath climactic rise and fall, until he had taught them new values.

Delian sonata melody continues the process. Although the ebb and flow of climax is the life-blood of the melody, neither

K

the disposition of climaxes nor the phrasing marked constitutes the form which, in Bergsonian phrase, is " a becoming ". In its happiest moments Delian melody has the seemingly unpremeditated strains of Shelley's skylark ; when it is weak, no formalities will disguise the weakness. Neither Delius nor Elgar gave interviews on " How I write ". They did not move in the so-called world of music and had no time for its tittle-tattle. Their methods must be deduced, a process easier with Elgar than with Delius, for Elgar expanded more traditional methods, and critics do not tire of discovering what he learnt from Brahms, Franck or Tchaikovsky. The mature Delius so transcended his inheritance from a different lineage that casual listeners could suppose him to be without musical ancestry. But an examination of the chamber works especially will prove that he fought a hard battle with problems of form, and often, when at second best, fell back on sliding sevenths, devices of repetition and sequence, the " six-four " of harmony and metre, or a sudden change of key or texture which drew attention from the general to the particular without justifiable dramatic significance. There is no need to gloss over the failures, but, in examining the chamber work, to see how a naturally great artist became a better craftsman.

There are still listeners who can let themselves " sag " ; the rich harmonies, especially in orchestral pieces, carry them away to the misty hills or dank woods, and they would worship a tone-poet whose art is too recondite for exegesis, too sacrosanct for inquiry. Their attitude is seen in a programme note to the 1929 Delius Festival :

" There never was a composer whom it is less profitable to discuss in terms of technique. For Delius, technique had not the smallest interest, *save as the means of expressing himself in music*." (My italics . . . and what better reason for interest in technique ?) " We cannot do better than approach this music from a similar angle, and open our hearts with reverence and gratitude . . . to one of the supremely great masters of music."

Let the opening words be altered . . . " There never was such a composer ". Will posterity open its heart uncritically ? How long will last the *allure* of the rich dominant ninths, elevenths and thirteenths, already at the finger-ends of every " syncopated pianist ", or of the descending chromatic bass known to every dance band ? They may soon lose their nostalgic powers and merely serve to allot to a certain work its date in musical history. In Delius the power even of these idioms will last in the fine conceptions which transcend the tricks of a period.

Chamber writing lays bare for inspection everything in a composer's basic methods, for it is unaided by the adventitious mystery of orchestral colour ; only the most spineless or extremely unusual music fails to survive the test of pianoforte reduction or of chamber restrictions. Even a Brangwyn fresco or a Persian carpet survives monochrome photography. Speculative thought is naturally ruled out of music, and when we say a composition conveys thought, we must mean that it shows some interest of counterpoint, rhythm, programme or form. If Delius chooses to be so highly melodic that such " thought " must flow in the course of the melody, we can compare that melody with its weaker relative — " blues melody ", which is usually lacking in strong intervals and rhythmic interest. It is short-winded, depending for its rhythmic pattern upon the recurrence of metrical pulse, as it depends upon the outworn devices of balance and sequence for its length. " Red-hot rhythm " is only the persistent repetition of one figure, rendered effective, if at all, by slickness of drummers or other performers. The red heat rarely lasts a season. We turn from such music to the phrasing and rhythmic interest of Examples 43 to 46.

Only in the 'cello sonata could even Delius maintain a rhapsodic flight commensurate with the work as a whole. In his " Sonnet upon the Sonnet " Watts-Dunton wrote : " A sonnet is a wave of melody ". The line is figurative as applied to the sonnet, but of the Delius 'cello sonata it would be literally true ;

there are barely ten bars of rest for the solo instrument and hardly a phrase of non-thematic origin. In examining the sonatas

Ex.44 FIRST VIOLIN SONATA

Ex.45 FIRST VIOLIN SONATA

Ex.46

FIRST VIOLIN SONATA

we may trace the strivings Delius made before he reached the perfection of the 'cello work.

Sonata for Violin and Piano No. 1 (1892)

This was Delius's second violin sonata ; the first was not published. Delius had fully found his musical language before the work under consideration was written ; there are no " periods " among the sonatas, only passages of success or failure. The opening is such a perfect and coherent rhapsodic flight that it could not lend itself to traditional metabolism without losing its life. It may be, and is, repeated, with varying harmonies and slight variations or extensions, to be judged according to their advancing the work coherently or not. The first tune (Example 44) being intricate and moving downwards, the second (Example 46) is rhythmically broad and mounts upward. Episodes of sometimes scrappy, cadenza-like bravura, make the variety. It is far more easy to make brilliant accompaniments to a repeating theme than to achieve the fourteen bars of cumulative rhapsody in the marvellous prologue-cum-epilogue found here. The feat has recourse to no dynamic mark beyond

mezzo-forte, for Delius works to a climax not of loudness but
of tension.   He is helped by being a good violinist himself.
Having reached the high, thin tones of the E string (Example 47),
poised there, he makes climax not with a savage scrape of the
higher notes but by an intense change, directed to be played on
the rich metal G string (Example 48).

Again, after the luscious harmony preceding, the piano makes
short prelude to climax with more strong, diatonic chords.

Although sensuously pleasant, the tune of the slow movement (Example 3) makes for poor joins.   Delius relies on the
fact that it is difficult to become tired of such a bird-like melody ;
but he falls back on a feeble attempt at augmentation (bar 1,
page 9 of score) and on cadenza tricks.

The main theme of the finale (Example 49) is developed on
almost classical lines in some places, with a little second subject
for contrast.   It has an almost Elgarian continuity, and the final

cadence actually suggests Brahms. Though one has no fault to
find with the development seen in Example 50, one quotes the
passage to show how, were it just at a slightly lower level, the
stuff would sound like lesson four in a course of " syncopated
pianism ".   It remains to explain the curious interpolation

marked " slow and mysterious " just before the final pages,
analogous in effect to the sudden solemnity of the chorale played
on the trombones at a similar point of Brahms's first symphony.
It cannot be dismissed as mere caprice ; the fanciful may either
find in it a solemn significance or liken it to the slumber of a
humming-top before its last dither and fall, or to the candle's
low burning before its final flare.   Whatever our reactions, the
grim contrast with suavity is artistically right.   Of the sonata as
a whole we may say, as of Elgar's first symphony, that though

it is less perfect than its successor, it has between its covers much of the composer's self-revelation.

Sonata No. 2 for Violin and Piano
  (Published 1924: edited by Albert Sammons and Howard Jones)

This work is better known than its predecessor, both as first written and as presented in the Tertis-Reeves transcription for viola and piano. A careless glance might make one think it more concise than the first sonata, for there is no break between movements. The first part settles without recapitulation to a short slow section that possesses no material of sufficient importance to be called a theme; the final stretch uses reminiscences of the first. But the sonata is by no means in clear sections with epilogues and bridges; a list of the tempo marks alone would show its diffuseness. Like other composers, Delius grew in pursuit of economy and coherence, and in this work we see transition from the prolix first violin sonata to the well-knit 'cello sonata. The extended rhapsody of the 'cello work rubs shoulders with efforts to apply a new treatment to the old Grieg-like themes. The tunes tend to be inherently interesting rather than productive of synthesis. One at least is thoroughly bad, precluding even decent harmonisation; the arpeggiated accompaniment does not deceive one into supposing that the chords themselves make an interesting sequence. This sort of thing is makeshift:

Ex.51

In the little tune which forms the germ of the middle section Delius unconsciously quotes the notes of the corresponding theme in the first sonata.   An excellent piece of development during the opening of the final section (Example 52) shows how

Ex. 52

one cannot judge a Delius chord sequence without considering the melody ; this can be tested by playing the accompaniment alone and noting how fine a passage is made with such commonplace material ; the conclusion of the sonata reaches unusual grandeur.

Sonata for 'Cello and Piano (1916)

Whether people choose to recognise the fact or not, this work is a masterpiece almost flawless in its perfection ; one uses the epithet after deliberation, for it denotes a coherence rare in many of this luxuriant composer's most enjoyable major works. He does not try to become symphonic in attitude but develops his unique " vocal " rhapsody to lengths (in the literal sense of the word) not seen hitherto in the sonatas or elsewhere.   It cannot be appreciated by reading the score, and even in performance it demands skilful nuancing. The tune, already quoted at Example 43, grows in curves of waxing or waning intensity, two or three anticipations of climax anticipating the main one — a point to be mastered by the sensitive player. Yet let it be once more emphasised that the *arrangement* of climaxes, either in time or on paper, does not constitute the form, which is inherent in the movement.

Heseltine writes :

> In looking through the manuscripts of Delius's early works, one is particularly struck by the fact that they display virtuosity of technique in the academic sense of the word. . . . The realisation that the form of a well-made work must necessarily be latent in its initial conception, even as the form of a flower is latent in its seed, is a slow and arduous process ; in the meantime the young artist learns to build with imitative scaffolding. Through formality he attains to form.

That might be a brief history of the sonatas.

The first and third sections of the 'cello sonata are complementary, the final pages making a beautiful recapitulation of the opening. The second tune of these sections stands out very clearly as belonging to a less rhapsodic type ; it is therefore treated in a more traditional manner, and the two types of technique make fine contrast.

Ex.53

The slow movement (Example 53) is full of that rich sentiment found in Delius and the lyrical parts of Arnold Bax's symphonies and tone-poems — a Celtic inheritance which is usually called " poetic " or " legendary ". The words seem vague, but they serve their purpose since they are universally understood ; they show the great difficulty one is faced with in writing about works of this kind. The 'cello sonata is not a piece to write about but to play and hear.

Sonata No. 3 for Violin and Piano (1930)

"It is remarkable how far he gets using the same old technique" ran a contemporary critique of this work. The orange is not dry, however, while good juice can be sucked from it. If the man has something to say, the technique is not despised, however outmoded. Yet one understands the feelings that prompted the remark. The critic talked of an ageing technique because he did not want to acknowledge an ageing Delius. The technique here happens to be more clear and economical than in previous violin sonatas, but the fire burns lower. Its beauty is of mellow reflection, not of impassioned rapture. The dictated works — the " Idyll ", the " Song of Summer " and this sonata, for example — can now be seen as the last utterance of a master whose life's tasks were drawing to their close ; no longer is he troubled with problems of form ; the pieces live on their intrinsic merits, but their glory is of an autumnal hue.

The movements are separated, each being as clear and coherent as a song. They sound much better than they look. The listener may be surprised, for instance, to find how easy it is to overlook the difference made by a well-held pause on the B flat in this passage :

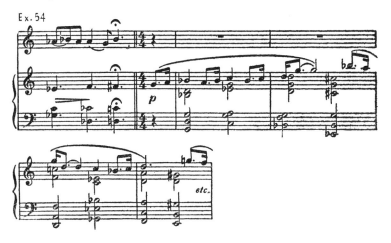

The B flat anticipated by the violin, and the pivotal D of the bass on both sides of the double bar, prevents a change which would be too sudden. Similarly one must not be deceived, in reading the score of the slow movement, to thinking that the effect in performance, with the sustaining pedal expertly used and with the accentuation given by Delius to notes most essential to the harmony, is unduly thin. A stiffening of cross-rhythm here would spoil the lightness intended. The change from dance to song and back again emphasises the harmonic richness of the dance.

The little song (after double bar in Example 54), being a fair example of Delian stock-in-trade, shows how different that stock is from other stock. It owes nothing to the French impressionists or the English folk-song school. Delius never wrote this sort of music :

nor this :

The difference lies in the intention. The impressionists, the sheep school, and the watercress school aimed at picturesqueness; " atmosphere " and scenic suggestion are pleasant in short spells, but Delius has the extra utterance which comes from the human heart. With him is no musical vegetarianism ; he belongs to the romantic main stream. The whole-tone chord may occur, a passage may proceed by parallel fourths, but there are no consistent limitations. He revels full-bloodedly in his musical materials.

Pieces for Piano

Five piano pieces.

Three preludes for piano (dedicated to Howard Jones).

Dance for harpsichord (dedicated to Mrs. Gordon Wood-house).

Delius wrote little for the pianoforte alone, and the pieces have small emotional range. It would be surprising to find that they were not " orchestral " had we not seen, in accompaniments to songs, that Delius could write for the piano. His treatment is neither percussive nor clumsy ; it is entirely harmonic, but only in the dance for harpsichord should that description be taken as the equivalent of " chordal ", and for this exception Delius had a good reason.

The pieces might be regarded as accompaniments without songs. They cannot compare in scope or quality with the sonatas, for Delius's thought, as we have seen, inheres in rhapsodic melody. Without it he cannot charge a work with deep feeling : it becomes a pastel. Unpretentious samplers (for they are no more) of Delius's writing for the piano need careful playing, as in giving the right weight of each note on the following cadence and effecting the perfect evaporation of the chord:

The pedal should not be applied till the second half of the first bar (see asterisk) or else the F sharp, which Delius did not tie over, becomes prominent.

The harpsichord gives no opportunity for lingering chords or for the glowing and fusing of colour ; Delius therefore does not break, tie or arpeggiate his chords, but presents them complete on every accent. They do not stand alone ; sometimes the upper fingers of the right hand provide a melody, sometimes the chords make the equivalent of a melodic sequence. Naturally the harpsichord dance is more liked than the preludes, and it is remarkable that an admirer of Grieg did not, in his younger days, write pieces for piano with a strong melodic interest.

Quartet for Strings (1916)
  (First quartet not published)

It is commonly believed that a quartet which strains beyond its limitations is bad. But who decides when a quartet does so ? Who does not admire the G minor quartet of Debussy or the D major of Borodin ? Does any composer who seeks colouristic effects rather than architectural grandeur write orchestrally ? To prove that this is not so, let us compare this very colourful quartet with the orchestral piece " In a Summer Garden ".

Both open melodically, but with what different expectations! The opening of the orchestral work is an entity (Example 58)

Ex.58

which could only be repeated, or decorated by new harmonies. It is therefore not one of the flowers in the summer garden ; it merely establishes a mood and is used — in the manner stated — towards the end of the piece, recalling the first mood. The opening of the quartet is no such static affair ; it is rhapsodic and cannot be isolated. It presages a long flight of flowing texture (Example 59).

Ex.59

The structural contrast is even greater. In colouristic music the tonal kaleidoscope frequently takes a sudden shift. There is no need to give a music-type illustration. Half a dozen good examples may be remembered from Debussy's " L'après-midi d'un faune ". One impression past, the scene changes. Delius was driven to it in the piano preludes, yet not in the harpsichord dance, whose tune gives continuity of construction. The quartet has no sample like this from " In a Summer Garden " :

Ex.60

Moreover the suspensions, even the chords, called by text-books " higher discords of the dominant ", have a certain carrying power, for the listener tends to resolve them mentally, or to anticipate their resolution. Even when Delius stays, in quartet as in orchestal poem, upon some apparently motionless, shimmering chord, he suggests poise rather than rest. Dr. Hull's text-book on modern harmony emphasises the difference between writing of men like Delius (though the composer is not actually cited) and that of the impressionists.   " A single chord makes an impression, which is less definite than a thought ; it needs a succession of diverse harmonies or notes to convey a distinct idea."   Therefore the impressionist composer will reproduce the same chord on different degrees of a scale for love of its impression.   (Of course, this language is entirely symbolic.) His chief mannerism consists in similar motion of chords from Hucbaldian fourths or fifths to dominant elevenths, and this is rarely found in Delius. An example quoted elsewhere by Dr. Hull comes from the introduction to the song " In the Seraglio Garden ", where Delius needs the effect.   Impressionist devices occur also in the piano preludes, including the favourite whole-tone chord ; but it has been already shown that, denied melody, Delius seeks only the effects of harmonic colour in the preludes.

In contrast with these notes on impressionist methods, here is Heseltine's account of Delius's musical texture, which applies perfectly to the first movement of the quartet. (One wishes that it applied to the last movement, but it must be bluntly admitted that the work should end with the wonderful " Late Swallows " movement rather than with the otiose and unworthy finale.)

One might almost say that the chord is to Delius what the note was to polyphonic composers, and that the melodic line is seen in a higher dimensional aspect of changing chords. . . . The principle of modulation, though not discarded, is pushed to the farthest extremity of chromatic licence and it is the continual shifting of the tonal centre that gives his music an elusiveness and peculiar quality of reticence. It imparts to every phrase a suggestiveness and hidden meaning that is never actually uttered.   Polyphony with Delius is not the *cause* of harmony . . . but its apparent effect.

The most satisfying parts of the quartet are those wherein Delius is true to his own fluid idiom. The scherzo departs from this,

and Heseltine's description will not apply to that movement
without forcing. The composer once more becomes traditional
rather than personal, but without any sign of incompetence. He
does not fall into the snare of over-spaced or over-thick chords,
which would spoil the tone of four instruments in their en-
deavours to get too many notes at a time. All is " apt for viols ".
Note (Example 61) how well the lower instruments are fused,

while the first fiddle stands apart with its tune at just the right
distance from the other parts.

Like the occasional classical scherzo with trio, the movement
contrasts a dance with a song, but as a whole it means much less
to the lover of Delius's music than does the lovely slow movement which follows.

" Late Swallows ", though pure chamber music, has the
effect of a tone-poem. Between a prelude steeped in autumnal
atmosphere, which returns at the conclusion of the piece, is
a masterly stretch of visual and aural suggestion, comparable
with " Summer Night on the River ". This has been called
" a sort of musical *pointillisme* ", the tune riding above and
below the shimmering chords as in the work for small orchestra just mentioned. To this type of texture we have seen
that Delius was very partial — the quiet middle section of
" Brigg Fair ", for instance, translates, in different mood, the
" Late Swallows " texture into orchestral terms ; in the quartet,
as will be seen from the example, the harmony is satisfactory

without the first violin, whose thin muted waving gives it what the title demands.

Why is this quartet neglected ? Merely because of a bad finale ? The rest should appeal more than other chamber works,

if only because of the evocations in the slow movement and the sensuousness in the first. The scherzo makes just the right contrast. Excluding the finale, there is not one incompetent piece of writing, one dubious or uncomfortable bar. If all quartets must be architectonic, then Delius has not written one. He has no mould ; the significant form is in the flower and foliage during its unfolding before us. A romantic, still more a rhapsodic, composer who triumphs over formal problems should have more credit than his classical brother who works to a model — unless that brother be one of the giants.

If Delius were not a great craftsman as well as a great artist, his work by now would be almost out of sight and out of mind. He sings of the transitory beauty of summer, the English summer that we still know. Will later generations know it ? The countryside is changing, and a harder music has come along with the beauty of machines, aircraft and white-tiled swimming-pools. " And I said : O that I had wings like a dove ; then

L

would I flee away and be at rest." If the time comes when hills, woods, lanes and hedgerows are utterly spoiled, when no man can find tranquillity undisturbed by something streamlined, moving by road, on water or overhead, the loveliness we once knew may be captured only as an emotional experience in the poetry of Keats and the music of Fred Delius.

CHAPTER THIRTEEN

DELIUS'S SONGS

ALTHOUGH many musicians think that Delius was not a great writer for solo voice with piano accompaniment, the songs should be given a whole chapter if only because he wrote them persistently throughout his career as a composer, exclusively of those he set with orchestra, or of the more song-like parts of operas. From 1885, the date of his first known composition, which was a setting of Hans Andersen's " Two Brown Eyes ", until his last illness, sets of songs appeared at intervals, as can be seen by a glance at the list of his works. More than any other of his writings, the songs enable one to find how much he owed to admiration of other composers, how long it took him to brew his own musical alchemy, how much his cosmopolitan tastes, especially in verse, made him musically eclectic or unstable (if at all), how far he was English and insular in expression, to what extent he was dominated by certain moods or images, and whether, on the whole, he was master of his mannerisms or they his master.

There are not enough songs to make Delius primarily a song-writer, but his instrumental work usually sings, and of his total output, the larger portion ncludes works for voices, solo, choral, or both, with orchestra. Criticism is mistaken when it asserts that he could not write for voice. The demands, in solo as in choral writing, are sometimes exacting in regard to range ; but it would be unthinkable, for instance, to give purely orches-tral versions of those works he wrote to include a solo voice. though we happily listen to transcriptions from Wagner's music dramas at our Monday night " Proms ".   In Delius's vocal scores human voice there must be — its tone, its distinctive appeal, its flexibility and its words.

Concerning words, one must defend Delius from the charge that he is a mere cosmopolitan of the Paris studios ; eclectic in taste he was, but nondescript-cosmopolitan never.   When he chose Norwegian verse, his heart was in his beloved Norway ; he was no dabbler in the language ; he was well steeped in its atmosphere and culture and, in consequence, his first sets of songs, the Five Songs from the Norwegian of 1888 and the later Seven Songs, are those in which whole passages show direct inspiration from Grieg, while others might be Grieg's own.   The songs from Shelley, Verlaine and Nietzsche show the same exclusive enthusiasm for the chosen poet and the " overtones " of his verse.   Delius's writing is always in agreement with the poetic inheritance of country, time and poet . . . the French songs being highly French, the English obviously English in spirit.   The Nietzsche texts, as indeed that of the " Mass of Life ", are treated in a way which reveal an English musician, but one absorbed in the German prose-poet.   That words fully filled his mind when setting them may be shown from the fact that the verses he chose were always those of contemporary, or very nearly contemporary, poets, men whose sentiments spoke for his own at this or that stage of his aesthetic growth and imagination.

In a fine series of articles upon Delius's songs (contributed to *Musical Opinion* (October 1936–June 1937) A. K. Holland speaks of the wide contrast between Delius and Wolf in treatment of words ; one presumes to quote at some length :

His aim is to distil just that poetic essence which resides not only in the immediate images of the text but in the very character of the language . . . his musical approach is, therefore, at the opposite pole from that of such a song-writer as Hugo Wolf, for whom the whole shape and method of the song are often dictated by the literary features of the poem and whose musical images seek their justification in their absolute congruence with the immediate verbal imagery. . . . Delius

is more concerned with creating a new psychic and emotional experience, for which the words of the poem are merely the framework.
The justification of his songs lies frequently not in the words so much
as in the emotional echoes to which they give rise. In Wolf the poetic
and musical elements are organised on the basis of parallelism and
they only " appear to meet ", to use an optical analogy. *In Delius
they actually do meet, indeed they are one.*[1] Wolf's accompaniments, for
example, are often complete in themselves. Delius's never are.

And again, later in the same article :

This does not mean that Delius was indifferent to questions of
verbal expression. . . . He did, in point of fact, take considerable
pains to achieve a declamation that was at once accurate and expressive.
It will be seen that, in his early songs, he was sometimes swayed by a
purely musical idea or rhythm which acted to the detriment of his
word-setting. But in his later songs he is often extraordinarily successful in achieving a balance between strictly musical and declamatory
values. . . . The greater part of his word-setting is syllabic and follows
the verbal stresses carefully ; only, the phrase as a whole is governed
rather by the poetic sentiment he desires to enforce than by the strict
pace and stress of the spoken phrase. It is only composers of ex-
cessively literary mind who confuse musical with verbal declamation.

Holland then classifies Delius's songs into five main types, but
in this short survey we may hold the view that the legendary
type, the idealistic or philosophical type, the love songs and the
songs of regret are all contained in or analogous to the main
classification — songs " in which a human emotion is set against
a background of nature-symbolism ". Is not this true of the
bigger conceptions, such as " Sea Drift ", " A Song of the High
Hills ", " Appalachia ", or even purely orchestral pieces like
" Brigg Fair " ? And did not Delius thereby go farther in this
direction than Grieg, to whom he owed so much both of manner
and method ? In certain songs and many piano pieces, Grieg aims
to express only some mood of nature itself, some picturesque
fancy or scene.

[1] Italics added in quotation.

Two Delian characteristics are plain in the first two published albums of Norwegian songs, which were composed in Delius's younger days. It was both in escape from Bradford and later as a free visitor that Delius saw most of Norway, and his first songs are dedicated to Nina Grieg. Foremost among the two characteristics mentioned is, therefore, debt to Grieg ; of a few dozen snippets to illustrate the obvious, two are given (Examples 63 and 64).

A mannerism to persist with Delius and inherited from Grieg, sometimes ineffective but more often enhancing appeal, was the use of echo-like refrains, especially at the end of a song. The fact that Grieg had himself set certain poems did not deter Delius from using them, apparently without offence to the older composer. The second characteristic to persist even in the best later songs, as indeed of greater works, was the approximation, in both literary sentiment and music, to plebeian songs and ballads, which seem only slightly more naïve and melodramatic in the kind of ditty sung at smoking concerts or musical family gatherings, such as may be overheard in passing down the street on New Year's Eve. Thus, the deservedly popular and not too Grieg-like " Nightingale ", from the first album, is at the same emotional level as a popular " Blackbird song " or " Down in

the Forest ", and perhaps the best song in the group is " Sunset ", the most sentimental.   Crude English translations accen-
tuate the sentimentality.

In the second Norwegian album, how near is the sentiment
of " The Minstrel ", still more of " Love Concealed " — sensitive songs that only a snob could dislike — to that of ballads
like " The Lute Player " !   And who is too sophisticated to
delight in the commonplace lilt and harmony of " Little
Venevil " ?

It should be pointed out that Scandinavian verse abounds in
the balladry of parlour songs, either directly narrative, or drawing sentiment from a situation of frustrated love.   The favourite
of the set is, deservedly again, " Twilight Fancies ", to a poem
of Björnson which had already been set by both Kerjulf and
Grieg.   Delius's evocation of the romantic situation and atmosphere is more finely achieved than by either predecessor, and
the refrain is beautifully used, especially when, at its last hearing,
it turns to a despairing minor cadence.

Ex.65

The first Delius settings of English words were chosen from
Tennyson's " Maud ", and formed the cycle used by other
English composers.   Delius would not allow their publication,
so their music cannot be discussed ; but it may be noted that
the words are those of balladry.   The glorious Shelley lyrics,
owing nothing to Grieg, are the apotheosis of popular love songs
of the more tempestuous kind.   Holland considers that even
Shelley's outpourings, in the light of subsequent debasement of

their literary currency, are fit only for what he considers "somewhat meretricious" Delius. The present writer, loth to give an opinion contradictory to Holland, finds the songs thrilling, and cannot understand why they should not seem so to anybody who recognises the level of their sentiment and seeks neither the rich restraint of Brahms nor the refinement of Fauré. For one cannot hold that Delius "writes down", or makes the unusually exuberant accompaniments out of other music than his own — not even in those climactic sections where the voice soars at full throat and the piano throbs its repeated chords and wide-flung arpeggios in honest-to-goodness ballad style. A measure of their advance on former songs is the difficulty of quoting, unless at length ; one suspects that the Shelley lyrics have found their way into homes wherein are no other Delius songs.

The "Indian Love Song" (" I arise from dreams of thee ") and "Love's Philosophy" are, in words and music, the direct outpourings of young infatuation ; they are not, therefore, respectable ; and even the slightly more restrained " To the Queen of my Heart" has no trace of courtly, melancholy or reflective love, nor of refined or profound love, only the ardour of headlong calf love. The three songs are unparalleled in Delius because nowhere else does he set words of the same type ; if the music is cheap — and I am sure that it is not — it is the complement of Shelley's language. As elsewhere, the composer perfectly absorbs the spirit of a chosen poet and verses.

In no change of manner does this absorption more wonderfully manifest itself than in the contrast between the Shelley and the subsequent Verlaine songs, the latter pleasing musicians of ultra-delicate palate. Along with " Il pleure dans mon cœur " and " Le ciel est par dessus le toit " of 1895 we may examine three later songs to words of the same poet, " La lune blanche ", " Chanson d'automne " and " Avant que tu ne t'en ailles ", the last written as late as 1919. The five are as consistently in one style as the praised or despised Shelley lyrics, yet at no particular

moment does one of them show identity with anything in
Debussy, Reynaldo Hahn or Fauré, being, to an English musician,
as distinctly French as any compound of them all. This may be
seen best by making points of contrast with music of the Norwegian and English songs — a slower pace, a greater number of
short passages wherein the voice sings part of a phrase on the
monotone (as in *Pelléas et Mélisande*), rising or falling a single
interval at the phrase-ending. Here, too, is no extreme ranging
of the voice, as in the soaring Shelley outbursts. The suggestions
and evocations of this poetry, exquisite in the limited as in the
fuller sense of the word, are perfectly captured in accompaniments which, though not to be mistaken for Debussyist pianism,
are much more " French " than any others in the Delius songs.
Nowhere else does Delius use the technique suggesting the rain-
drops in " Il pleure dans mon cœur " (Example 66), the summer
sky in " Le ciel est par dessus le toit " (Example 67), the chaste

Ex. 66

O bruit doux de la pluie par terre et sur les toits

Ex. 67

moonlight in " La lune blanche ", or the soft winds of the fading
year in " Chanson d'automne ", or of inward rapture at the
birth of a flaming dawn in " Avant que tu ne t'en ailles ". These

are held by many people to be Delius's most perfect, though not most characteristic, songs. They, more than others, need the words to be known and followed, yet their perfection is apparent if the poems are not understood. So much of assonance and " word music " is there that there could be too much music from the wrong composer ; had we not proof to the contrary, we should have thought Delius the wrong composer. As it is, even the limited range of the voice is an asset instead of an imposition, for the singer can dwell upon each syllable and inflection without preoccupation with other matters than the poem.

Collections of songs from the Danish comprise one or two whose accompaniments were subsequently scored for orchestra. From 1897 came " Irmelin Rose ", " In the Seraglio Garden ", and " Silken Shoes ", all by Jacobsen ; three other Jacobsen settings were made at intervals from 1901, including " Wine Roses ", " Through the long, long years " and " Let Spring-time come ". The other Danish songs, " The Violet " and " Autumn ", are to verses by Holstein, a minor nature lyricist. Jacobsen (1847–85), though belonging to an older generation than Delius, was a favourite with the composer. His novel *Niels Lyhne* provided the story of the opera *Fennimore and Gerda*, and a Jacobsen poem the words of " Arabesk " for baritone, chorus and orchestra.

Few of the Danish songs are very well known, a fact that may be attributable to Delius's efforts to make new departures in song form. He shuns former strophic methods except in two settings, one of which, " The Violet ", is noticeably weak, whereas the other, " Irmelin ", is exquisite. Haunting variants

Ex. 68

Ir-me-lin rose,   Ir-me-lin sun,   Ir-me-lin love-li-est of all ____

of its refrain (Example 68) express the hopeless love of the many suitors who approach the cold-hearted and mocking princess.

Delius's striving to set the other poems as through-composed songs gives passages of fine dramatic effect, as in the Holstein ballad " Autumn " ; or flights of beautiful rhapsody, as in " Silken Shoes ". In " Summer Night " the vocal part alternates between declamatory recitative and arioso. Yet only two of these settings, the luscious " Wine Roses " and the poignant " Let Springtime come " — a difficult song of changing moods — achieve satisfactory coherence. It is strange that, in essaying the new method, Delius was unable to make well-knit pieces of the very short verses " The Violet " and " Silken Shoes " ; both seem to tail off, and in neither is the content fairly clinched and well rounded. Of the whole bunch only " Irmelin " and the exquisitely languorous and perfumed " In the Seraglio Garden " are likely to become established in the repertory.

One would expect the four Nietzsche songs of 1898 to show Wagnerian influence, and in their exclamatory masculinity they do recall the mutual greetings of heroes to be found in parts of the *Ring* cycle. But the harmonic colouring, the fascination of nature, especially in the seascape of " Towards new seas ", make them unmistakably Delian. The translations are weak, but lovers of Delius at once recognise the brave defiant aspirations, properly for the baritone voice to which they are set, which fired the composer whenever he used words of Nietzsche or Whitman. The quality is here as surely as in " Thou will unbending " from the " Mass of Life ", or " Joy, shipmate, joy " from the " Songs of Farewell ".

In the first Nietzsche song, " Towards new seas ", the joyous adventurer sets off to a new world which may be a terrain or, as usual in Nietzsche, some nebulous, radiant vision of the *Ewigkeit* ; and the spirit of this song is maintained in the other three, notably in " The Wanderer " and " The Wanderer to his Shadow ". Delius's wanderer is in adventurous quest, not dejected like the wanderer of Schubert. The appeal of Nietzsche in Delius's mind has been fully discussed elsewhere ; suffice it here to repeat that the philosophic teachings are of no import except as implicit in the hero's reflections and defiances — nearly always, be it noted, in the contemplation of land, sea, or sky in one of nature's more glowing or impressive aspects.

The remaining songs, written a whole decade later, are to English words. Some people consider them the best. They are gloriously headed by the short, intense setting of W. E. Henley's "The nightingale has a lyre of gold", the loveliness of which reaches perfection in its wonderful ending. Fiona Macleod's "Hy Brasil" tells of the western isles of Celtic legend where sea and stars meet, and where light and life are eternal; the radiant tranquillity of these Hesperides of heart's desire is hauntingly captured in the refrain "Come away, come away", and Delius's use of a characteristic Scottish rhythm cannot but be intentional.

Two years later (1915) come the three Elizabethan lyrics — Nashe's "Spring, the sweet Spring", Herrick's "To Daffodils" and Ben Jonson's "So white, so soft, so sweet is she". These may be considered along with the setting of Shakespeare's "It was a lover and his lass", composed the following year. Since these verses have lured so many composers and are likely to lure others, Delius's entirely personal treatment is remarkable. They were penned at a time when most English musicians were interested in Elizabethan music and trying to catch its spirit, sometimes with pseudo Tudor and modal sophistications. Moreover, Delius's friend Heseltine was foremost among Tudor scholars, his editing and commentary being almost unmatched in vividness and scholarship. Yet Delius, while capturing the spirit of the poems, nowhere evokes the music of his English contemporaries in their dealing with Elizabethan lyrics. It is said that he took no interest whatever in antiquarian research; without scruple he makes these poems into modern Delian songs. As to whether he was justified let passages like the following tell :

Ex.69

The hey-nonino spirit is not revealed in " It was a lover ", which Delius treats in a cynical way. Whether this is faithful to Shakespeare it is hard to say, but of Delius's intention there is not the slightest doubt, for it is in the refrain itself that the intention is most evident.

CHAPTER FOURTEEN

NOTES ON HIS MUSIC IN GENERAL

THESE notes are necessarily scrappy since it was thought wise to discuss any characteristic of Delian idiom when a particular work, especially one requiring a quotation in music-type, gave opportunity. Much has been said in the foregoing pages, for instance, concerning Delius's harmony, for surely it is by his harmony that his music is most easily recognised.

Delius's scores are liberally covered with what the text-book calls accidentals, but Delian harmony differs from that of most previous composers in that the sharps and flats are not accidentals, and that his music is chromatic only in the literal sense — " coloured ". The difference between Delius's conception of one of the rich chords, founded on a dominant root, and the same chord as used by one of the older masters, may be seen if we consider how the boy picked up that harmony which he declared was a gift of nature. One feels that it was not a gift ; all that nature gave was the ability to absorb and identify (not necessarily name in technical terms) the harmony in such music as he heard. His sister and others tell us that he used to sit at the keyboard and clothe some simple tune, like " Annie Laurie ", with the magic harmonic colours we meet in his orchestral settings of tunes like the plantation song in " Appalachia " or the folk-song in " Brigg Fair ". From what source came these chords ? Were they original ? Of course not. Their use by Delius was, for those days, original. Suppose that, in some music by his favourite composer, Grieg, he came across a chord

like this, which has been freely arranged from Grieg's piano
concerto, though we could have found it in many another piece
by Grieg :

Delius was a sort of musical gourmand in the matter of harmony,
and we may suppose that, liking the chord, he tried it on every
note of the piano thus :

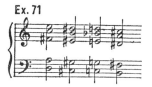

We can hardly say that the sharps and flats needed to write that
cascade of chords are chromatic alterations of plain chords, or
notes in melodies which would otherwise be written in a plain
scale, as are the accidentals put into the little tune which over-
rides the chords in the Grieg extract.   What is more, the chords,
or rather the various placings of the same chord, are used for
their own effect ; they are not connected by any harmonic progression.   In the Grieg example they are, for the note " A " is
pivotal to both chords.   Delius does not " modulate " (that is,
pass from one basic home-key to another) so often as does many
a composer whose music paper contains a far smaller number of
sharps and flats, but, as Heseltine has said, " the chord becomes
in Delius what the note was to older masters, and a chain of
chords are often used like a chain of notes ".

In his improvisation of accompaniments to songs, such as
delighted his school friends at Isleworth, his slidings up and

down the keyboard may have been in the simple stage seen at Example 71, which looks like the sort of thing the jazz pianist does when sliding a tune into a different key. In fact it is from Delius that commercial composers, wanting " blues " harmony for dance music or films, have quarried much of their material. Ephemeral music follows in the wake of fine musical invention, and we hardly see a travel or wild-nature film without hearing echoes of Delius in its music. We need follow his career as a composer only a short way to see him using his harmony with better discrimination than do these imitators. Looking for a use of the particular chord quoted, one finds the following in an early and not very distinguished song :

No doubt many improvising musicians could use the chord twice in succession almost as well as that, but when the song was written the idiom had distinction. If we dip up the same chord in any of the masterpieces of Delius's maturity or old age, we find still greater discrimination and taste. Here is the same chord, made more beautiful by the suspended D sharp (see asterisk) in *A Village Romeo and Juliet* :

and with what lovely effect it is struck by the harp in the closing
cadences of the " Walk to the Paradise Garden " :

Finally here is the chord used just for its own rich sake in the
last of the masterly " Songs of Farewell ", written just before
Delius's death (see asterisk) :

It will be noticed that, as Delius writes better, his once-
cherished chord is part of a spate ; the music flows instead of
sagging or sliding.   Sometimes this means, as in the excerpts
given at Example 73 and Example 74, that notes in the chords
are also members of tunes which flow and interweave hori-
zontally, but Delius's champions exaggerate the horizontal movement of his parts.   It does not make his music in its totality any
better or any worse than Elgar's that his single instrumental
parts are not so interesting to an orchestral player as are the other
man's.   If we judged a texture on the interest of linear parts
we should think little of a brilliant orchestrator like Rimsky-
Korsakoff, who may give his double basses nothing in the course
of a movement but a pizzicato stroke on main accents and on the
same two or three notes.   But the rich chords, like the one we
isolated for study, are technically discords, whose discordant
notes should be resolved.   Had Delius acquired them academic-

M

ally he would have reached them through the flow of parts. That is why highly chromatic work by other composers who use the same chords, let us say Wagner in *Tristan*, Schönberg in " Verklärte Nacht ", or Strauss in *Rosenkavalier*, sounds so different from Delian texture.   When young Delius found, chiefly in Grieg and Chopin, the chord he liked, he disregarded the passing horizontal flow of " resolution " and ripped it *en bloc* from its context.   Thus Grieg's song " A Swan " ends with this cadence :

We can imagine Delius finding it, arresting it, extracting it, and trying it up and down the keyboard :

What has been a suspension or an ornament becomes a chord in its own right.   Perhaps the best-known examples of this are those badly overworked harmonies, the " added sixth " and the " added second ".   If one strikes middle C with the E two notes above it and the G two notes farther up, one has the C major triad.   The most common of decorations among the older masters was the suspended sound of the A next above, which resolved its then-called discord by coming down to G.   Delius strikes all four notes together, thus adding the sixth from the C to the triad ; and if there are enough Cs and Gs in the lower octaves he strikes the D farther up, thereby adding the second.

One of Delius's best-used and worst-used mannerisms is the holding of these chords for a long time with different instruments oscillating, say, between the A and the G, or the D and the C, thus making a quivering texture. Instances will be seen quoted at Example 4 and Example 8. A beautiful extreme case is the inclusion of a high B, the seventh of the scale, in the major chord of C which opens " On hearing the first Cuckoo in Spring " (see Example 13). Some of the loveliest, most spell-bound moments in his works are those in which the music seems motionless but breathing ; the texture is just alive, its heart throbbing on one of these quiet chords.

The persistency of a composer's mannerisms has nothing to do with his stature as an artist. One particular idiosyncrasy may be used a thousand times and move us profoundly at the thousand and first ; another may only irritate at its ninety-ninth appearance. We have seen that Delius began with chords and worked to textures ; it is almost certain that he acquainted himself with his harmonic materials chiefly while moving his hands up and down the keyboard of a piano ; yet he did not take the trouble to learn good playing or to know the feel of good piano writing. As a result it cannot be denied that those mannerisms which do spoil his music, not *because* they are mannerisms but because they are used to " carry on " where nothing more purposeful has been suggested from within the composer, are derived from this chordal approach to harmony and from the habit of improvising at the keyboard.

The trick of " sagging " or sliding in sevenths, ninths, elevenths, or whatever the chords are, or in a mixed string of those chords, puts Delius at an uninspired moment no higher in artistic level than are commercial composers. But it is not just harmonically that Delius sometimes lets himself go " on tap ". Ernest Newman once spoke of the " persistent six-four ", by which at first one supposed he meant the six-four chord held " motionlessly " as just described, not the six-four time-signature. Yet it is true that too often Delius is lured into a triple tempo, and lets its metrical oscillation serve for the genuine organic movement which he cannot recapture until the access of a musical idea forces rhythmic invention ; and it is at such a weak rhythmic moment that he is likely to fall back on his lush harmonic stock-in-trade. When these manner-isms were new, Delius's admirers were intoxicated by their sheer richness, and it is interesting to notice that, whereas Heseltine repeatedly eulogises the first Dance Rhapsody or " Appalachia ", modern critics point to " Sea Drift ", which is sparing of the luscious harmony and which has great rhythmic diversity, if not austerity, as one of the most thrilling of his masterworks.

We must be careful, however, not to condemn Delius merely because some of his most characteristic materials have become debased and used by every theatre and dance band. To do so would be to align oneself mentally with the silly young man one recently heard declaring that he would not go round the corner to hear a Beethoven symphony " which was a mere reiteration of tonic and dominant chords, served up loud or soft ". Who's a-deniging of it, Mrs. Prig, except the word " mere " ? The Delian mannerism, or even his ordinary harmonic procedure when not inspired, shows itself for the weak thing any technique is when used without express purpose, far more quickly than does Beethoven's much more simple harmony when heard without Beethoven, as in the operatic overtures of one of his German or French imitators. There are two reasons for this ; the first is the richness of the Delian materials, for " lilies that fester smell far worse than weeds " ; the second is the absence of academic scaffolding to make transition between the better music and over the inferior.

The free methods of form are neither superior nor inferior to the academic ; either a work has organic life or it has not, but no method ever gave the life. In his queasy rebellion against school practices, Delius saw no vitality in works which used devices of contrapuntal imitation, or " development " of thematic articula. The people who cannot feel the superb form of the " Siegfried Idyll " or " In a Summer Garden " are no more dull, though they may be more prejudiced, than those who hold that there is necessarily waste matter in a work which uses the architectural symmetry of sonata form, with its main sections based on sequence of keys. Of course Delius had a right to his own tools, and we have a right to declare when he fumbles with those tools, for he must have known it himself. No doubt fumbling at the keyboard was a refuge to hide weaknesses, just as in certain quartets Brahms fumbles with the classical busy-ness. But a high standard of self-criticism, such as Mozart, Beethoven or Brahms possessed, can leave the best workmanship, the best academic carpentry and joinery, in sterile transition passages. The composer who has no desire to use the scaffolding must expose what sags for all to recognise and criticise. He cannot deceive the musically simple ; the classical formalist can, and is first exposed by a professional critic or connoisseur.

We should not generalise about formal procedures, unless we are certain that another departure would have served the composer's purpose better than the one he used. For instance, Mozart's C minor fugue is a glorious failure not because there are too many entries of the subject or its inversion, but because they are wrongly timed and put into too small a space. The teacher is wrong who says " The full imitative sequence of a phrase should normally not be made more than once directly following the phrase, or at most twice " ; in twenty of Wagner's most inspired passages — Siegfried's journey to the Rhine, Isolde's Death Song — or in Delius's " Walk to the Paradise Garden ", a phrase may be repeated sequentially a dozen times and hold the interest, stir the emotions, each time ; it is the unlucky thirteenth which we deplore.

Delius's own advice to other composers should not be taken without reservations. It may be summarised : " Have no

theories. Examine those of others, including the academics, and
see if there is anything that interests you. Write only what you
like and as you feel." Such advice would be of use to another
Delius who, living in the last stage of a technical period, was
sufficiently great to push its decadent technique one stage farther
and give it, almost solely in his own music, a glorious autumn
or Indian summer.   When told to write *as they felt*, his over-
powered disciples naturally felt — or thought they felt — as *he*
did, through *his* technique. But our examination of a few sample
chords shows that his technique is a terminus ; those chords are
all related to a key centre, to which they yearn. Remove the key
centre, as one would by extending his means, by adding notes
to the chords more thickly than he did, and no longer could
one obtain his effects, his expression. Faced with such an
impasse, the young composer *must*, at first, experiment with
theories. Delius declared that he had no theories : nonsense ;
he may not have formulated them in words, but his selection of
materials at the keyboard was done by a theory, as certainly as
was the selection made by Scriabin, Schönberg or Stravinsky.
What Delius himself did not know was his own size ; he said
he had no theories because his creative urge was greater than
his interest in the means with which he created. Otherwise
neither he nor Beethoven, for that matter, would be included
among the great artists of music.

Delius therefore felt towards academic musicians as Somerset
Maugham feels towards Walter Pater in the following passage :

It is strange that I ever admired that prose. It does not flow.
There is no air in it. A careful mosaic is constructed by someone with
great technical skill to decorate the walls of a station dining-room.
Pater's attitude towards life about him, cloistered, faintly supercilious,
gentlemanly, donnish in short, repels me. Art should be appreciated
with passion and violence, not with a tepid deprecating elegance that
fears the censoriousness of a common room. He is an example of a
type in the literary world that is common and detestable — the person
who is filled with the conceit of culture.

Perhaps that is why Delius had no great interest in the dainty French school of composition which, since it used Delian materials in an un-Delian way, one would expect to have fascinated him. He saw the limitations of others ; he does not seem to have been aware of his own.

His range of expression certainly was more limited than that of most composers who reached his place of honour. This is compensated by the supremity of inspiration within his own artistic range. Cross the frontier and the fall in level is huge. In how many works, for instance, does he give us a " laughing chorus " to the words " Ha ha ha " or " La la la " ? In every one of the operas published, in the " Mass " and in the " Requiem " ; and how often is such a chorus convincing either as the laugh direct, the laugh preliminary, the laugh oblique or the laugh prefixed by any other of Mr. Puff's epithets ? Instead of attempting to make a case for Delius's versatility, we should say gratefully, as did a critique of the violin sonata dictated to Fenby : " It is wonderful that he gets so far, using the same means ". His operas show his spiritual limits very well. He could not, like Wagner, have made the diverse beauties of *The Ring, Tristan, Meistersinger,* and he had not a trace of Mozart's psychological versatility in catching character, mood or situation ; even in scene painting, he was equalled by the Italian " verismo " composers. The latest film composer could crack you a better storm, roar you a better brawl, raise you a nastier smell, or coo you a soppier reconciliation than could Delius. But dawn, sunset, the hills, the sea, with humanity as the sapient and feeling crown of nature, the longing of men and women to be always their " higher ", more mystical, more dionysian, more clairvoyant selves, their yearning to fulfil their love passions and their craving for beauty, for identity with the strength and glory of creation, together with their mastery of its pain and evil, or as Delius would have said, their longing to be able sincerely to " yea-say " nature and their own nature —

the expression of these things is, in vulgar parlance, "right up Delius's street".

The vulgar phrase has been used purposely, because cultured and uncultured in the usually accepted sense of the term have an equal chance to experience these aspirations and longings through Delius's music. It is ordinary folk, not professional musicians, who have decided that Delius is a great musician. This declaration is not a smug *securus judicat* ; it postulates no theory about the Democracy of Art. Mozart's place of honour was never more secure than it is to-day, but we may doubt if two-thirds of his latest devotees can discriminate between great Mozart and period Mozart ; their awareness of his master-strokes increases with their growth in general and musical culture. Delius can appeal greatly to people of general, as distinct from musical, sensibility. Yet Delius was one of those people who " detested the herd " and despised the man whose philosophy, Christian or not, was based on the love of all others as oneself, the love of Mrs. Smith with her limited, genteel intelligence, Mr. Brown with his plebeian manners and cheerful philistinism, and little Tom the Piper's son who is an official of the Church Lads Brigade. Delius was no Franciscan. Detestation of the " herd ", which should have nothing to do with political sympathies, is usually the result of fear ; and though any intelligent person regrets, fears, and fights the more stupid and ugly expressions of herd thinking and herd feeling, a man who has been more fortunate than another in acquired gifts of birth, privilege and education, or in natural gifts of brains, health and artistic sensibility, and then says, " Others rail at the herd : I merely ignore it ", is rudely and offensively cutting himself off, excluding himself from the category of inferior humanity, though retaining in that category the company he addresses.

Those who have been most powerful in their influence over men, from Buddha and Jesus to Shakespeare and Beethoven, have spoken to be understood by all humanity, and have often identified themselves with the poorest, humblest, least gifted of their fellow-creatures. As a man, Delius sometimes behaved and spoke with the exclusiveness which he never showed as an artist, and one has not failed to declare it, since it is the biographer's privilege and duty to put into temporary abeyance the rule " Judge not ". He was not ungracious or snobbish, but he had the defects of his class and age, his companions and his environment, which he raised into principles during the formulation of muddled Nietzschean thinking. Despite his contempt of the " herd ", he was probably most happy when among schoolfellows or the demi-rep company of Montmartre. Though he was never desperately poor, he was happier during his more impecunious days than he was after he had surrounded himself with all he loved in the house at Grez. He might or might not have been a greater artist had he known the delights of Hampstead Heath, but most probably he would have been just what he was. He is not a Beethoven, but what lives in his work, and what lives in Beethoven's work, is whatever transforms the humblest and weakest of sensitive listeners among the herd and puts him with the gods. He called it the " Dionysian spirit ", but it has an older and more abused name — inspiration.

CHAPTER FIFTEEN

CONCLUSION

THE course of musical history would have run almost as it has done if Delius had never been born ; he had a certain influence over his younger contemporaries, but Delian technique without Delius is a snare, seeming to lose even its characteristic voluptuousness. We have seen in our critical survey that the greatest of Delius is to be found in the great pantheistic choral works, the loveliest of Delius in the orchestral nature poems, and a vindication of his craftsmanship, his knowledge of other materials than those to which he normally limited himself, in his songs and chamber music. Even so, we have not found out *why* he fascinates us ; we know only *how* he does so.

We may find some answer by comparing him with Debussy, whose influence was considerable. Technically Debussy is brilliant, more brilliant than Delius ; imitation of his work could harm no student ; it would stimulate, whereas Delian harmony would enervate. In orchestration alone, Debussy's " La Mer " is a more vivid piece of pictorialism and a more virtuosic piece of writing than Delius's " Sea Drift ". Why, then, do many regard " Sea Drift " as one of Delius's greatest works ?

If we judge Delius as we should judge Debussy or Strauss, we should call him inferior to either of them ; they set out to depict, one delicately, the other grossly ; they succeed. Delius does not set out to depict but to communicate. He is not a painter in sound, despite the titles " Summer Night on the River ",

"A Song of the High Hills", etc. What he evokes comes incidentally to our minds while we are receiving what he has to communicate. Much of the evocation is done by the listener. Were the clarinettist to miscount his bars so that we heard no cuckoo notes in Delius's best-known work, its effect on us would be exactly what it is now.

In other words, Delius had the temperament of a mystic, one who uses symbols. It seems strange to stress the religious nature of a man who attacked orthodoxy and institutional religion, and there may be musicians who, responding to the mystical symbolism of Palestrina or Bach, or to the associations of Gregorian chant, are unwilling to call Delius mystical, even though they use the word Cecil Gray applies to his muse — "dionysian". For the mystic, phenomena are symbols ; falling leaves are a symbol of death, the sunrise a symbol of resurrection. By this definition, we may see the difference between Debussy and Delius, or Strauss and Delius. "Tod und Verklärung" gives only a morbid picture of the sick-room and death-chamber ; we smell corruption, hear the death rattle and envisage a Hollywood conception of blissful futurity. But the midnight of Zarathustra, for all its highfalutin nonsense, gives us a spiritual *Verklärung*, just as "Sea Drift" brings us to the mystery of death and bereavement. "La Mer" is a series of brilliant seascapes ; "Sea Drift" makes the moaning of the ocean surge an occasional background and commentary upon the general rhythm of resigned grief. Debussy's "Fêtes" is a far more brilliant evocation of its subject than is "Brigg Fair", but the latter is the work of a seer, a visionary.

Patmore said that mysticism is incommunicable to those who have not experienced it. One may add a corollary : mysticism is difficult to communicate by unfamiliar symbols . . . those not previously associated with spiritual experiences. A man spiritually moved by Vaughan Williams is merely disgusted by Mahler ; another wonders how Mahler, having used "Veni Sancte

Spiritus " in the first half of his most ambitious work, should turn to the closing scenes of *Faust* for the second. Many Englishmen recognise the greatness of Goethe's work aesthetically but cannot call their response to it by the name " mystical experience ". Wordsworth gained his revelation of divinity through nature ; to Blake " nature is a hindrance ".

England has been insular in her mysticism. Medieval England had her devotional mystics, such as Julian of Norwich and Richard Rolle, and the succession of Catholic mystics has included Crashaw, Francis Thompson and Hopkins ; the Anglican Church, retaining liturgy, episcopacy and ceremonial, has produced a rich harvest of devotional mystics among such poets as Donne, Herbert and Vaughan. Blake, though not an ecclesiastical type, is a devotional and religious mystic, using much of the traditional symbolism. Of this type of mystic, England boasts no Teresa, no Pascal, no Boehme, no person to compare with the great Jesuit fathers. Nor has she produced philosophical mystics to be ranked with Plato, Kant or Descartes ; but of *nature mystics* she claims some of the greatest, in a succession which includes not only poets, although few of her poets have failed to show some streak of nature mysticism. Many an Englishman who may be an orthodox churchman, who may regard as nonsense Wordsworth's theory that contemplation and communion with nature can make a man good, secretly finds granted to him when in quiet communion with nature a revelation which is denied him in the liturgy and symbolism of orthodox practice. Such a man, I believe, was Delius ; and such he remained when the tenets of Nietzsche *seemed* to voice his own ideas.

There are obvious likenesses between Delius and Wordsworth. Both were hard-headed north-country men, with acid tongues upon occasion. Both disliked indirect forms of expression, including classical formulae in art ; the opinion of the poet, that verse should use language understood by unlearned men, would have been endorsed by the composer had he written musical manifestoes. Very often have critics applied to Delius the Wordsworthian dictum that poetry is " emotion recollected in tranquillity ". The phrase seems suited to the composer of the " First Cuckoo ", the haunting cadences of which could be hummed by an unlearned man after a first hearing. Yet there is never any " writing down ", no conscious imitation of rustic or popular song, for Delius, like Wordsworth, had an arrogant, aristocratic nature. It is not, then, because he evokes a specifically English countryside, that Delius appeals so much to English folk ; it is because he has a specifically English vein of mysticism. Like Vaughan the Silurist, he has but to communicate what he remembers in tranquillity, to evoke our Thames or Avon as Vaughan did his beloved Usk, though Delius's river was in France.

Where, then, does Delius differ from Wordsworth ? By having the temperament only, not consciously following the mystical way. It was not the *beauty* of nature that Wordsworth sought but the *life* in nature, and, like devotional mystics, he stressed the need for purgation and discipline. The Nietzschean Delius would have repudiated such a demand ; he worked hard enough as an artist, but his attitude to nature was consciously hedonistic and only temperamentally mystical. He has the same sense of infinity, of " the boundless opening from finite experience into the transcendental ". To Wordsworth, even as a child, the disappearance of a road into the horizon was

> Like an invitation into space
> Boundless, or guide into eternity.
>
> (*Prelude*, Bk. 13)

In Delius, we are aware of " boundless distance ", of a human mind at one with the life in nature, seeking the horizon. Since his attitude to nature was hedonistic, since he followed no discipline of mystical vocation, his expression of " the boundless " more often takes the form of voluptuous longing for the beyond than of a Wordsworthian vision of the beyond, but the words of Nietzsche or Whitman made him seek the vision with an aggressive and adventurous masculinity.

In such music, the music in which he does not allow himself to sag, Delius much resembles another English mystic who was almost his contemporary — Richard Jefferies. This fact is obvious to anyone who hears " A Song of the High Hills " soon after re-reading *The Hill Pantheist*. Many an English boy knows Jefferies only through that wonderful childhood favourite, *Bevis : the Story of a Boy*, or perhaps through *The Gamekeeper*. Had Delius read these books at just the right stage in his development, and had he sought other writing by Jefferies, especially *The Story of my Heart*, his reading of Nietzsche while on a holiday in Norway would not have seemed such an extraordinary revelation. Underhill says of Jefferies :

A thrilling consciousness of spiritual life through nature, coupled with passionate aspiration to be absorbed in that larger life, are the main features of Jefferies' mysticism. This central Life Force, which he seemed at moments to touch, he refused to call God, for he says that deity is the purest form of mind, and he sees no mind in nature. It is a force without a mind, " more subtle than electricity, but with no more feeling than has the force that lifts the tides ".

Delius was aware of this fuller life and found ecstasy, if not vision, in the contemplation of nature. He spoke of his experience as being only emotional ; he would have declared that he made no effort of the soul but of the imagination. But he was religious *malgré lui*. No man without vision could, in the extreme of weakness and pain, dictate the exhilarating valediction of his last choral outbursts, the " Songs of Farewell ".

" Joy, shipmate, joy ! Pleased to my soul at death I cry ! "

APPENDICES

CATALOGUE OF WORKS

Key to publishers

A.   = Augener
F.   = Forsyth
Sch. = Schirmer
T. & J. = Tischer & Jagenberg (Leipzig)
U.   = Universal (English editions either Winthrop Rogers
          or Boosey and Hawkes)

A number of Delius's works are also reprinted by Oxford University Press. The publishers given in this catalogue are the original printers.

DRAMATIC WORKS

Date of Composition		Publisher
1890–92	*Irmelin.* Opera in three acts. Text by the composer	
1893	*The Magic Fountain.* Opera in three acts. Text by the composer	
1895–97	*Koanga.* Opera in three acts, with prologue and epilogue. Text by C. F. Keary from material in G. W. Cable's novel *The Grandissimes*	U.
1900–1	*A Village Romeo and Juliet.* " Lyric drama in six pictures ", in performance three acts with prologue. Text by Jelka Delius from Gottfried Keller's novel	U.
1902	*Margot la Rouge.* Opera in one act. Text by Mme. Rosenval. Lithographed but not published	
1908–10	*Fennimore and Gerda.* " Music drama in nine pictures." Text from J. P. Jacobsen's novel *Niels Lyhne*	U.

INCIDENTAL MUSIC

1897	*Folkeraadet (Parliament),* satirical play by Gunnar Heiberg	

1920   *Hassan ; or the Golden Journey to Samarkand,*   U.
       verse drama by James Elroy Flecker

CHORAL WORKS

1902   *Appalachia.* Variations for orchestra and chorus.
       Version for orchestra only composed in 1896
1903   *Sea Drift.* Baritone, chorus and orchestra. Text U.
       from Walt Whitman's " Out of the cradle end-
       lessly rocking "
1904–5 *A Mass of Life.* Soli, chorus and orchestra. Text U.
       from Nietzsche's *Also sprach Zarathustra*
1906–7 *Songs of Sunset.* Soli, chorus and orchestra. Text U.
       by Arthur Symons
1907   *On Craig Dhu.* Unaccompanied chorus. Text by U.
       Arthur Symons
1908   *Midsummer Song.* Wordless, unaccompanied U.
       chorus
       Wanderer's Song. Unaccompanied male voice U.
       chorus. Text by Arthur Symons
1911   *Arabesk.* Baritone, chorus and orchestra. Text by U.
       Jacobsen
1911–12 *A Song of the High Hills.* Orchestra and wordless U.
       chorus
1914–16 *Requiem.* Soli, chorus and orchestra. Text by U.
       composer, from Nietzsche
1917   *To be sung of a summer night on the water.* Two U.
       unaccompanied wordless choruses
1924   *The Splendour falls.* Unaccompanied chorus. Text O.U.P.
       by Tennyson
1930–32 *Songs of Farewell.* Chorus and orchestra. Text U.
       from Whitman

VOICE AND ORCHESTRA

1888   *Paa Vidderne.* Recitation with orchestra. Words
       by Ibsen
1889   *Sakuntala.* Tenor and orchestra. Words by
       Holger Drachmann
1898   *Nachtlied Zarathustras.* Baritone and orchestra. U.
       Afterwards incorporated in " A Mass of Life "

1907   *Cynara.* Baritone and orchestra. Words by   U.
       Ernest Dowson
1925   *A Late Lark.* Tenor and orchestra. Words by   U.
       W. E. Henley
1930   *Idyll: Once I passed through a populous city.*   U.
       Soprano and baritone with orchestra. Words
       by Whitman

SONGS

1885   *Two Brown Eyes* (Hans Andersen)
1888   Five Songs from the Norwegian   A.
       Slumber Song (Björnson)
       The Nightingale (Welhaven)
       Summer Eve (Paulsen)
       Longing (Kerjulf)
       Sunset (Munck)
1889–90 Seven Songs from the Norwegian   T. & J.
       Cradle Song (Ibsen)
       The Homeward Journey (Vinje)
       Twilight Fancies, or *Evening Voices* (Björnson)
       Minstrels (Ibsen)
       Secret Love (Björnson)
       The Bird's Story (Ibsen)
1891   Song cycle from Tennyson's " Maud "
       Come into the Garden
       Go not, happy day
       I was walking a mile
       Birds in the high-hall garden
       Rivulet crossing my ground
       Three Shelley Lyrics   T. & J.
       Indian Love Song
       Love's Philosophy
       To the Queen of my Heart
1895   Two Verlaine Songs (published with three other   T. & J.
       Verlaine settings) :
       Il pleure dans mon cœur
       Le ciel est par-dessus la toit
       A third song, " Plus vite, mon cheval ", with-
       drawn from circulation

1897	Seven Songs from the Danish :	
	Let Springtime come (Jacobsen)	T. & J.
	Irmelin Rose (Jacobsen)	U.
	In the Seraglio Garden (Jacobsen)	U.
	Silken Shoes (Jacobsen)	U.
	Wine Roses (Jacobsen)	
	Through the long, long years (Jacobsen)	
	On the seashore (Drachmann)	

The three of these songs published by Universal are included in the album of " Five Songs ", together with the two Danish songs written in 1900

1898	Five Songs, including the Nietzsche settings :	U.
	The Wanderer and his Shadow (Nietzsche)	
	The Lone-ganger (Nietzsche)	
	The Wanderer (Nietzsche)	
	With Joy we journey laughing (Drachmann)	
1900	Two songs from the Danish :	U.
	The Violet (Holstein)	
	Autumn	

Published in the album of " Five Songs " :

1901	*Black Roses* (Jacobsen)	T. & J.
1908	*The Nightingale has a Lyre of Gold* (Henley)	T. & J.
1910	*La lune blanche* (Verlaine)	T. & J.
1913	*Hy-Brazil* (Fiona Macleod)	T. & J.
	Two songs for a children's album :	Sch., O.U.P.
1915	Three Songs :	U.
	Spring, the sweet spring (Nashe)	
	Daffodils (Herrick)	
	So sweet is she (Ben Jonson)	
1916	*It was a lover and his lass* (Shakespeare)	U.
1919	*Avant que tu ne t'en ailles* (Verlaine)	

CHAMBER MUSIC AND PIANO SOLO

1892	Sonata for violin and piano (unpublished)	
1893	String quartet (unpublished)	
1896	Romance for 'cello and piano	
	Romance for violin and piano	
1915	Sonata for violin and piano (published as No. 1) (begun in 1905).	F.
1916–17	String quartet	A.

1917	Sonata for 'cello and piano	U.
1919	Dance for harpsichord	U.
1924	Sonata for violin and piano (No. 2)	U.
	(Arrangement for viola and piano made by Lionel Tertis)	
1930	Sonata for violin and piano (No. 3)	U.

ORCHESTRAL WORKS

Concertos :

1890	*Légendes* (Sagen) for piano and orchestra (unfinished)	
1906	Concerto for piano and orchestra in one movement (first version, 1897, in three movements)	U.
1915–16	Double concerto, voilin, 'cello and orchestra	A.
1916	Concerto for violin and orchestra	A.
1921	Concerto for 'cello and orchestra	U.

Tone-poems and rhapsodies :

1888	*Hiawatha.* Tone-poem	
	Rhapsodic variations (unfinished)	
1892	*Sur les cimes.* Tone-poem (after Ibsen)	
1895	*Over the hills and far away.* Tone-poem	U.
1899	*Paris : The song of a great city.* " Nocturne "	U.
1907	*Brigg Fair : An English Rhapsody*	U.
1908	*Fantasy : In a summer garden*	U.
	A Dance Rhapsody (No. 1)	U.
1911	*Life's Dance* (revision of *The Dance goes on*, 1898)	T. & J.
1913–14	North Country Sketches :	A.
	Autumn : The wind soughs in the trees	
	Winter Landscape	
	Dance	
	The March of Spring — woodlands, meadows and silent moors	
1916	*A Dance Rhapsody* (No. 2)	A.
1917	*Eventyr (Once upon a time).* After Abjörnsen's folk-lore	
1918–19	*A poem of life and love*	
1930	*A Song of Summer* (using material from " A poem of life and love ")	U.
1932	*Irmelin Prelude*	U.

SMALL ORCHESTRA

1912	Two pieces for small orchestra :	T. & J.
	On hearing the first Cuckoo in Spring	
	Summer Night on the River	
1915	Short piece for string orchestra	
1918	*A song before sunrise,* for small orchestra	A.
1925	*Air and Dance,* for string orchestra	U.

MISCELLANEOUS

1886	*Florida.* Suite for orchestra	
1888	Two pieces for orchestra :	
	Marche caprice	
	Schlittenfahrt	
	Pastorale, for violin and orchestra	
1889	Little Suite for orchestra. March, Berceuse, Scherzo, Theme and Variations	
1893	*Legend* for violin and orchestra	F.
1897	Norwegian Suite, for orchestra (incidental music to Gunnar Heiberg's play *Folkeraadet*)	
1925	Caprice and elegy, for 'cello and orchestra	U.

BIBLIOGRAPHY

Beecham, T., *A Mingled Chime*.   Cassell.

Blom, E., *Music in England*.   Penguin Books.

Cardus, N., *Ten Composers*.   Cape.

Delius, C., *Frederick Delius*.   Ivor Nicholson & Watson (London).

Dyson, G., *The New Music*.   Oxford University Press.

Fenby, Eric, *Delius—as I Knew Him*.   Bell (New Edn. Quality Press).

Gray, C., *A History of Music*.   Kegan Paul.

   A Survey of Contemporary Music.   Oxford University Press.

   Peter Warlock.   Cape.

Heseltine, P., *Delius*.   Bodley.

McNaught, W., *Modern Music and Musicians*.   Novello.

GRAMOPHONE RECORDINGS OF DELIUS'S MUSIC

(A) THE DELIUS SOCIETY. Each volume contains seven discs. The orchestra is the London Philharmonic. Cond. Sir Thomas Beecham.

Vol. 1 :

Paris
Eventyr
Closing scenes, *Koanga* (London Select Choir)
Interlude and Serenade, Act. I, *Hassan*
Two Shelley Songs (Heddle Nash)

Vol. 2 :

Sea Drift (John Brownlee and London Select Choir)
Over the Hills and far away
In a Summer Garden
Intermezzo, *Fennimore and Gerda*

Vol. 3 :

Appalachia (B.B.C. chorus)
Closing scenes, *Hassan* (Van der Gucht and Covent Garden chorus)
Prelude, *Irmelin*
La Calinda, *Koanga*

(B) SEPARATE RECORDINGS available in 1946 :

Air and Dance. } *Two Aquarelles.* } Boyd Neel and Orch.	DECCA X. 147
Brigg Fair. L.P.O., cond. Beecham	COL. L. 2294–5
Brigg Fair. L.S.O., cond. Toye	H.M.V. D. 1442–3
Hassan, Intermezzo and Serenade. Hallé Orch., cond. Lambert	C. 3273
Koanga, La Calinda. Hallé orch., cond. Lambert	H.M.V. B. 8819

Indian Love Song.⎫
Irmelin   ⎬ Nancy Evans   DECCA F. 5707

Love's Philosophy. Isobel Baillie   COL. DB. 2378

On hearing the first Cuckoo. L.P.O., cond.
  Beecham   COL. L. 2096

On hearing the first Cuckoo. L.P.O., cond.
  Lambert   H.M.V. B. 8819

On hearing the first Cuckoo. L.S.O., cond.
  Toye   H.M.V. E. 505

A song before Sunrise. New Symph. Orch.,
  cond. Barbirolli   H.M.V. D. 1697

Summer Night on the River. L.P.O., cond.
  Beecham   COL. L.B. 44

Violin Concerto (Sammons). Liverpool Phil.
  Orch., cond. Sargent   COL. DX. 1160–2

Walk to the Paradise Garden. Royal Phil.
  Orch., cond. Beecham   COL. L. 2087

Walk to the Paradise Garden. Hallé Orch.,
  cond. Barbirolli   H.M.V. C. 3484

Walk to the Paradise Garden. New Symph.
  Orch., cond. Toye   H.M.V. D. 1738

(List kindly supplied by the E.M.G. Gramophone Co.,
11 Grape Street, W.C.2.)